OUR WARTIME DAYS

THE WAAF IN WORLD WAR II

OUR WARTIME DAYS
THE WAAF IN WORLD WAR II

SQUADRON LEADER BERYL E. ESCOTT

ALAN SUTTON PUBLISHING LIMITED

First published in the United Kingdom in 1995
Alan Sutton Publishing Ltd · Phoenix Mill · Far Thrupp · Stroud
Gloucestershire

British Library Cataloguing in Publication Data

Escott, Beryl E.
  Our Wartime Days: WAAF in World War II
  I. Title
  940.548141

ISBN 0-7509-0638-3

Library of Congress Cataloging in Publication Data applied for

The author and publishers are grateful to HMSO and the MOD for permission
to reproduce their photographs, © Crown Copyright/MOD.

Typeset in 12/15pt Bembo.
Typesetting and origination by
Alan Sutton Publishing Limited.
Printed in Great Britain by
Hartnolls, Bodmin, Cornwall.

CONTENTS

1
HOW WE CAME INTO THE WAAF

The 3rd September 1939 was one of the craziest days of my life!

Reporting to Royal Air Force station Stanmore Park, with my bottled specimen for a Medical, we were shown air-raid shelters, but told not to use them since they were full of water. If shelter was needed, we were instructed to take cover under sandbagged petrol pumps! Then we were despatched to the Gas Centre for masks. I was still trying to reach the Medical Centre when we were ordered on Parade.

At 1100 hours, the Station Commander appeared to tell us that war had been declared, and looking at the WAAF very severely he said, 'I will have *no* panic. Do you hear? I will have *no panic*!'

This was how Sylvia Swinburne of the Women's Auxiliary Air Force – the WAAF – began work with the Royal Air Force (the RAF) on the outbreak of the Second World War.

Eager young women were already queuing up to volunteer for the services. Posted on Recruiting at Air Ministry, Mary Scott commented:

Any airwoman who was in London during the Battle of Britain, especially in September 1940, will never forget it. Daytime German raids, in which a friend and I watched the dogfights in the sky over Regent's Park and the terrifying night raids, during one of which shrapnel pierced the water main at Victory House, and we WAAF (then sleeping in bunk-beds in the basement) had to race down to Adastral House to sleep, if possible, three in a bed.

At the end of February raids were trailing off a little, but in fact the two largest raids were still to come – April 16 and May 10 1941, during which we sheltered under heavy sideboards and tables in a private deserted house near Marble Arch. Very tired after a heavy night's bombing, we used to pick our way through the debris – chaos everywhere. Staff all were arriving late owing to long detours by buses. People were packed like sardines, sleeping in almost every underground station. When travelling, we had to make our way between the bodies.

Despite these conditions, or perhaps because of them, volunteers still continued to flow into Mary's office, prompting this reaction from her:

> If, when you're tired from a night of Blitz,
> You can with calmness face a day of Hits;
> If you can interview the whole day long,
> And never tell the customer she's wrong,
> But with an equal courtesy decline,
> Recruits of seventeen and ninety-nine!!!
> If, as you search for queries everywhere,
> To find the one you want just isn't there;
> If you have sent a draft of sixty-three,
> And Brighton sends some more just after tea –
> 'Have they their Dentals with them?' you enquire.
> 'Oh no,' they say. 'We threw them on the fire.'!!!
> If you can gently send them home again,
> And see them safely on the Brighton train;
> If, through it all, your friends go home at five;
> And if, by then, you find you're *still* alive –
> You can be sure, beyond all shade of doubt,
> That you're at Victory House.
> Be wise. GET OUT!

She was quite right about ages! Until 1941 it was 18 to 43, then extended to 17½ to 44, except for First World War WRAF. 'During my posting to Brighton,' affirms Ivy Chatsfield, 'I served under the oldest WAAF SNCO – Flight Sergeant Stalker. She had also served in the First World War and was by then nearly 70 years old.' Nor was it too unusual for a girl to slip in underage, as Cynthia Thompson did. She added two years on to her age because 'at that time birth certificates were not required, so I was able to declare I was 18 and 2 months.' Others borrowed the documents of a sister. 'One particular girl', remembers Winifred Smith at Sealand, 'was only 14. When he found out, her father said she had made her bed and she could lie in it! We taught her how to wash and iron, and always someone was close to keep an eye on her. We taught her right and

Raw recruits ('rookies') ready for their first posting – Sealand, September 1941 (Winifred Smith)

wrong where men were concerned. She was a charming girl when the war was over.'

There was a rather elderly lady, recalls Edna Murray, 'the tartar of all WAAF Officers – well past her prime! When she headed our Parade, she was always changing step, and we would do likewise. On passing the stationary band, they always changed the tune to "The Old Grey Mare Is Not What She Used To Be!" Was it a coincidence? I doubt it! But a titter used to run through our ranks and it made our day!'

The WAAF were all volunteers until 1942, when National Service for women was introduced. Joan Arnold made a note of 'Our Song':

> Ten bob a week,
> Nothing much to eat,
> Great black shoes,
> And blisters on our feet.
> We *volunteered* . . .!

The majority still continued to be volunteers afterwards, though they and the National Service girls did not always get on well together.

In 1943 Jean Leggat, a 36-year-old, and a friend of a similar age, joined an intake of 18-year-old conscripts from the north of England. 'I well remember one girl announcing to everyone, "Eh! We've got two bluddy volunteers with us!"' Nevertheless, WAAF Recruiting regularly exceeded its targets throughout the war.

Flight Sergeant Bungie was a liver-and-white spaniel who always accompanied Barbara Lecky, as the WAAF mascot, on her many Recruiting Drives.

> He had been taught by children to do the Scout Salute, which turned into 'Saluting for the King', and 'Dying for His Country'.
>
> He was given to me and grew famous for his tricks on platforms when I was making Recruiting speeches. I think he recruited more RAF and WAAF than I did. He flew everywhere with me and was completely air-minded!
>
> Many and varied were the reasons why girls joined the WAAF: Barbara Barrow 'enlisted in August 1944, in a fit of patriotic fervour, after seeing a film in which Veronica Lake, as an army nurse, blew herself and a Japanese truck to bits with a grenade. Fortunately I was not called upon to do the same thing!' Sheila Jollie joined 'because my boyfriend was a pilot, shot down in the Battle of Britain and killed. I also wanted to do my bit to serve

Flight Sergeant Bungie, WAAF (with his owner) salutes the King (Barbara Lecky)

my country.' [This was an often expressed comment.] Laura McGeown 'felt guilty being a civilian, enjoying the comfort of a well-run home with plenty of domestic help. I had attended a co-educational school and was distressed by the number of my classmates killed in the war. I felt that joining the WAAF was a revenge, in a small way, for their deaths.'

The majority, except at the start of the war, joined the ranks as airwomen. Promotion, if it ever came, was on merit.

Basic Training started in November 1939. Life for the young WAAF recruit began with her journey to her WAAF Depot. The location of these depots changed numerous times, sometimes because of heavy bombing nearby, but more often because numbers outran the accommodation, as intakes rose from hundreds a month to thousands per week.

With her friend Nancy, Irene Wright applied to join the WAAF at the Recruiting Office, Liverpool. 'We both passed and were eventually given rail warrants to travel to our first camp. What excitement and trepidation! Neither of us had travelled so far out of Lancashire before. It was a new way of life and a whole new world!' 'My first adventure came en route', says Florrie Phillips:

When the train stopped at Swindon, we were told there would be plenty of time to get out for a cup of tea. While we were drinking it, the train started off and had to be stopped some yards out of the station for us to rejoin it. We found that the only way to get into our carriage was to walk along the line and climb over a coal heap. Then we were locked in to prevent fraternization with the soldiers in the second part of the train. Not much Women's Lib then!

It was a different sort of arrival for Nicky Kelly. She turned up at Bridgnorth

driving a 1929 Big Six Racing-Green Bentley, called Oscar, with twin outside-straps across the bonnet and the Scottish Lyon talisman, denoting participation in a GB Road Race. So, having two hefty suitcases in the back, instead of the usual one, I bump-bumped my way up to the Guardroom on the hilltop, expecting the Depot to welcome me with open arms. Clearly the Service Policeman at the gate, mistaking the trappings of affluence, sprang to attention and gave me a smashing salute. I handed over my pink recruiting summons and a complete somersault resulted. 'You a recruit in that bloody thing?'

Arrived at Air Ministry in a taxi to impress! (Specially drawn by David Langdon from 1941 original)

Just then a station bus disgorged its WAAF occupants, so I was directed to 'Get lost with that lot.' Another SP, who helped me close up the car, sensing I was for it quietly told me to 'Get that bloody car out of sight – it will be a millstone round your neck else.' Good advice I discovered!

On arrival at the building where they were to be housed during training, there were more surprises in store. Pamela Anderson found herself sharing a hut 'with Charlotte the harlot and Gwennie the whore from Liverpool Docks. They had lice, but were very interesting as people and broadened my home horizons a lot.' Having set out with such excitement, Irene Wright commented:

Not only washing and changing in front of absolute strangers, but, talk about a new world, I thought we had landed in a real den of iniquity! There was this girl, sitting yoga fashion on her bed, absolutely naked, and brushing the longest black hair I had ever seen. She casually greeted the two boggle-eyed 'rookies' [new WAAF] – calm, cool and completely poised, quite unperturbed at our acute embarrassment. It later transpired that she was a top London model and had set her sights on driving the top brass around in huge limousines.

The beds inside a barrack hut ready for Daily
Inspection (DI). Note the heating stove in the
foreground (MOD)

The poster in the reception area at Bridgnorth stuck in the memory of Elizabeth
Woodin. It read: 'Homesickness is like seasickness – it soon wears off.' However
true this might have been, it still took time, as Joyce Williams realized. 'Fellow
trainees – a mixed bag. Lights-out on first night brought sobs from all directions.
Fatigues consisted of washing-up for hundreds. Drilling by female instructors
with blistering results. Successful Clerk SDs considered snobs by others.'

On her first night Nicky Kelly, after the episode with her car, was by now
'acutely aware that I was not welcome to all concerned. I shuffled off, heavy with
supper and exhausted, to the blanket, huts and my temporary bed space, until
numbered, kitted and documented, I was disposed of, into the heavy hands of
anonymity, which apparently was determined to get me by the scruff of my neck
and shake me into submission.'

To most girls the following days were confusing, to say the least. Whatever
Jessie White and her friends were later to become,

at Innsworth we were all very much scared 'rookies', and walked about in a
daze. All the recruits seemed to go about in bunches, signing here, checking
up there and getting odd bits of uniform issued to us. The place seemed alive
with Corporals and Sergeants, and without exception, they all pulled us up
for something. We tried our best to avoid anyone with stripes and after we

had our caps issued, to be on the safe side, we saluted everyone who was not one of us. Fortunately, this only lasted for about four days.

Service clothing – kit – from being virtually non-existent eventually trickled in during the first war year, but thereafter it increased vastly, to the great joy of some girls who had never seen so many lovely things in their lives. The collection procedure in the Clothes Store resembled a huge conveyor-belt system and took a very long time. The underwear was so ancient that it might have seemed out-of-date even in the First World War (when WRAF also served). In many a hut afterwards, the girls paraded it amid gales of laughter. Some items were described by Cherry Symonds:

> I was then handed something that made my eyelids flicker.
> Was it Grandmother's left-offs? No! My winter knickers!
> Corsets with bone and vests tied with tape . . .

Then, for good measure, she puts in a few other recognizable things:

> A camouflaged ground sheet, a glam'rous rain cape,
> Then added a necklace, not quite so rare,
> Two [identity] discs on a thin string, which now I must
>   wear.

Choosing to go into the WAAF rather than university, poor Beryl Nicoll made a fatal mistake. 'No one explained to me that the kit we were given on joining was not my own [but government property on loan]. When the first Kit Inspection came round, which meant nothing to me, I cheerfully told the Officer that I had sent all the awful underwear – especially the corsets – to my mother, who had put them in a jumble sale.' You can guess the horrified reaction, when speech returned!

Other things that the girls had to grow accustomed to were the peculiar RAF terms and names, such as Daphne Allison mentions:

> I've learned to 'bind', to 'pass the can',
> To 'shoot a line' with any man,
> To 'take a dim', to 'take a good',
> To answer either 'white' or 'wood';
> 'Tear off a strip', 'get in a flap',

Collect 'the gen', 'put up a black';
And all the same, I'm glad to say,
I don't regret a single day.

Louie McGaughey remembers:

the word 'ablutions' was unfamiliar to us when we first reported to Innsworth.
The first day there, we had a very long lecture about rules and regulations,
correct procedures and so forth, from a WAAF Corporal, and before she had
finished we were all getting a little restless. Finally one brave soul went up to her
and whispered in her ear. 'Right,' said the Corporal, 'does anyone else have to
go to the ablutions?' There was a dead silence. 'In other words,' she explained,
'does anyone else have to go to the washroom?' A sigh of relief ran round the
room and every hand was raised!

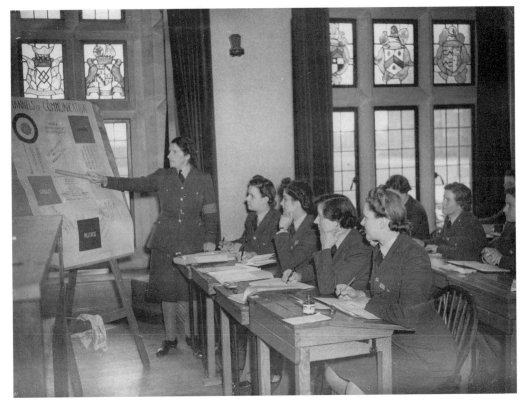

Classroom training – Loughborough, 1941 (Jean Holme)

Others were no wiser and very innocent! 'Nineteen years old and as green as grass', was Joan Burland's verdict of herself at that time. 'We had a talk by a WAAF Medical Officer and she told us that the WAAF had the lowest ratings in VD. I was furious to think that the other services were better than us!'

Learning to march bulked large in a recruit's life – not least, in the early days, because this was one of the few lessons about which their instructors were certain in a very new service!

In September 1939, before WAAF Depots existed, Eva Carmichael and those with her,

had no uniform, so wore our civvy clothes – hats adorned with flowers and feathers, high-heeled fashion shoes, silk stockings and kid gloves. We were ordered to attend a Parade in a large hangar, where we went to receive instruction on saluting and drill . . . To swing the arm up and salute proved disastrous to the hat brigade, but the march round the hangar was a shambles! The louder the Flight Sergeant roared, 'Left, right, and swing those arms', the more confused the mob became. The man approached one airwoman and said, 'Just step off with your left foot and swing your right arm forward'. She smiled sweetly at him and said in a loud voice, 'It's alright for you, ducks, but you see I can't do it, because I'm left-handed'.

While Joan Hey's Flight was on the move, their Flight Sergeant would bellow, 'Dig in them bloody heels and swing them bloody arms – they won't drop off!' 'We were creased with laughter. His vocabulary was very limited, but ours increased enormously!'

Winifred Smith remembers how homesick she felt on the train:

Then, on our first day we had drill, or as we called it 'square bashing'. Well! What sketches we must have looked! Our WAAF Sergeant was very good. She didn't bark at us unduly. In fact, we all liked her. She gave instructions very clearly, except, 'Pick up your dressings'. The confusion when she said that! Everyone looked at their shirts. I'm sure she must have been just dying to laugh! We finally got that sorted out.

However, not all Drill Instructors were so considerate. The male Warrant Officer with Sheila Jollie's entry was, 'very tough and sarcastic. He used to say, "If anyone wants to faint, now is their chance"! Quite a few girls were very unhappy and so went home – we were all volunteers in 1940!'

She was quite right, of course, as girls were enrolled and not enlisted at that date. They were really civilians in uniform, free to go whenever they wished, if only they had realized it, until the passing of the Defence of the Realm Act on 25 April 1941.

In retrospect, Irene Park sympathizes with the Drill Sergeants.

Not an enviable task with everyone sailing off in different directions. What it was like for the unfortunate instructors, I can't imagine. Probably it was a stock threat to RAF Sergeants. 'If you do/don't do this . . . you'll be posted off to one of the WAAF Depots to drill recruits.'

At the first WAAF Initial Training Depot at West Drayton, Sylvia Swinburne found that,

the baths were housed in a corrugated iron shack with a foot gap between the

Training staff off duty at West Drayton, summer 1940 (Kay France)

walls and roof. Under each bath ran a water gulley. The heat of the bath (when there was hot water) condensed on the roof, and showers of ice-cold water descended on one's bare back – an exhilarating experience to say the least, as was walking in the snow of that winter to them. We were drilled by a Sergeant and Corporal from the Guards. They would set us doing knees-up, bend, or some such activity, leaving us doing it while they went for a smoke.

Maggie Swarbrick recalls another menace at Morecambe: 'Early morning PT on the front, much to the delight of the many elderly men, who promptly filled all the benches to watch us bending and stretching, dressed only in our shirts tucked inside our regulation knickers – passion killers – incidentally the only time we ever wore them.'

All this exercise made recruits hungry, as Irene Park noted:

We entered the Cookhouse armed with our irons (knife, fork and spoon) where we ate as quickly as possible from the one plate provided, and

Massed WAAF recruits give a Physical Training Display at Morecambe in 1941 (the Instructors are in the front row) (Jean Holme)

hopefully before various dishes met in the middle – jam from one side, and kidneys perhaps floating across from the other side. One's implements were 'washed' in the murky trough. The mind boggles at the level of hygiene here, but no doubt the germs were hard put to it to survive in such spartan conditions. We did!

As to these culinary attractions, Mabel Payne discovered a strange fact:

The food? Well, we ate it! How strange. I used to *hate* liver and onions, and only started eating them since joining! It was because we were taken on a route march by a not-too-bright Physical Training Corporal, who lost the way. The march extended from two miles to nine. As a result we were *very* hungry on arrival, and to me, liver smelled like manna from heaven.

Another of the training hurdles that had to be negotiated and overcome was what was thereafter to become a regular Medical Inspection, called the FFI or a Free From Infection test – some said it was against 'scabies, babies and rabies'. It was really to check on such conditions as pregnancies, head lice and venereal diseases. The first examination usually came as a nasty shock to recruits, amusingly described by Cherry Symonds in a much longer poem:

> All shapes and all sizes stood there in the nude,
> Some moaning and groaning, 'Oh! Isn't this rude!'
> We then marched on further, still raging a storm,
> And sat ourselves down a hard wooden form.
> It was while sitting there, with our better halves bare,
> That somebody picked and turned over our hair . . .

'The recruits were on parade for jabs and chest X rays', recalls one of their Sergeants, Peggy Westwood. 'The whole morning had been spent taking airwomen in various states of undress to waiting doctors or nursing orderlies. After a while, I think, we all acquired a glazed look as the numerous shapes and sizes passed by. Then quite suddenly a Corporal, in a stage whisper, said, "May the Good Lord preserve us from suet pudding for lunch!"'

The doctor's examination was an ordeal which had to be undergone, both before girls could enter the WAAF as well as afterwards. A very shy girl, Joyce Gripton, 'having always been so fit that I had never visited a doctor', found that 'the strict medical I had before joining up gave me such a fright, and I was so embarrassed when my sample was called for, that I gave it from the cold water tap. It must have been clean as I was passed A1.'

Another facet already mentioned was the test for head lice, again before and after recruitment, about which Mary Scott wrote an interesting poem:

> There was a family of Nits, who lived upon the hair,
> Some sat upon a dark head and some sat upon a fair:
> Billy Nit preferred the blondes, he thought them such a lark,
> But Jimmy said the redheads got the most fun after dark!
>
> Round Mother Louse's knee they sat, and this is what she said,
> 'Now choose your site most carefully before you make your bed.
> Snuggle in among the curls. Use your imagination!
> And hide away before they take you to the Cleansing Station.
>
> You'll have a lot of sex appeal when you grow to a louse,
> But while you're just a little Nit, keep quiet as any mouse.
> Stick to your hair through thick and thin, whate'er your victim's fate,
> And your l'il girl won't catch the train today to Harrogate!'

When their training was over Doreen Gaskin and her friends celebrated passing their exams by painting the WAAF Sergeant's bike:

She had been particularly nasty to us! We went to a hangar, got all different colours of paint and did a grand job. Next morning we were amazed to be marched before the WAAF Officer for this offence, because we wondered how they knew it was our hut. Later we saw the trail of paint that led to and from the hangar and the bike, right into our billet. She was a jolly good Officer, laughed and after a few words, dismissed us.

At last came the day of triumph – The Passing Out Parade! Lilian Hetzel's took place on Morecambe Promenade:

The weather was dull, overcast and the wind was up to about 25–30 knots – very strong. The Air Force Band was playing and we were all marching in good time. Then the wind started playing havoc with our hats. I think mine came off first and, believe it or not, I didn't falter in my step and neither did the eight or nine girls who had lost theirs. Needless to say, when we were finally dismissed our Training Officers were beaming, and, yes, some fellow RAF members had gallantly recovered *all* the hats!

Trade Training courses usually followed Basic Training, and in the Blackpool billet to which she was sent while she did her Wireless Operators' course, Janet Knox encountered something unexpected:

We had only been there two days when my friend Jean was covered in spots. She reported to the Medical Officer and was told they came from bed bugs, but they couldn't move us until we had caught one to prove it. There followed a ghastly time when we had to set the alarm at 2.30 a.m., and then switch on the light and try to catch them in a matchbox. We succeeded in the end, and I can remember sitting on a Blackpool tram, clutching the matchbox and thinking, 'I bet the woman next to me would have a fit if she knew what I've got!'

Later, when we marched along to the Derby Baths, we were all lined up outside and the Sergeant shouted at the top of her voice, 'Fall out the girls with bugs!' We were then marched off for special Dettol baths, hair washing etc. – the whole lot associated with delousing! And when you think of the lovely, respectable homes we'd all come from, too!

Such experiences were liable to put off all except the least faint-hearted. Monica Hughes 'felt many times like giving up during my two weeks of training – some of it quite a shock to the system – but I was prevented on receiving a letter from my father, with Air Ministry in the Shetlands, saying how proud he was of "his little girl"! What could I do? I stayed.'

Something similar happened to Kathleen Wilkie. 'On mentioning in my letter home that my feet were very sore, my Scottish mother sent my train fare and said, "Just come home if you don't like it, dear." My father, an ex-Company Sergeant Major in the First World War, nearly passed out! I did not come home, of course!'

However, life on a Training Camp did have its compensations. At Wilmslow in the summer of 1943, Meg Bradford sums it up. 'It was a happy camp – 450 airwomen and 4,000 airmen!' Of course things could go wrong, as when Betty Ingle 'was detailed to take a bucket and brush and clean the ablutions [never popular!] "Those over there", said the Sergeant, pointing. I plodded over swinging my bucket, pushed open the door to be faced by a number of airmen in the altogether. I don't know who got the greater shock!'

Such shocks were not always one-sided either, as Dilys Upton narrates:

At Innsworth, a girl in a nearby hut awoke one morning to find someone in the next bed wearing a moustache. She screamed. The whole hut woke, including one very surprised and embarrassed airman. He made a hurried exit. Later a girl was heard to remark that it was pity he hadn't chosen *their* hut – they wouldn't have let him go so easily!

Nevertheless, the best feeling that the fledgling WAAF took with them from training was a strong sense of togetherness and friendship – something which outlasted the years.

As a privately educated, finishing-school type, Josephine Goldie-Scot was 'mixing for the first time with less privileged girls. I arrived with a group on the eve of my

The NAAFI, the social centre of a station. At the back, left, is the queue for tea (char) and sandwiches or buns (wads) – Wilmslow, 1945 (Kay France)

nineteenth birthday, so no possibility of cards or presents. But those kind-hearted strangers contributed ¹/₂d each and took me to the camp cinema and a snack at the NAAFI [the Navy, Army and Air Force Institute which provided food, plus social and leisure facilities, in a special building for all ranks of the Forces]. I've always considered that to be the best birthday present I've ever had!'

After training came the great adventure, when all the 'rookies', many still nervous and shy, were torn from the arms of their new-found friends and sent arbitrarily to their first, *real* RAF camp! Joan Dingwall captures the initial stages:

It's 1942 and our first posting! Get out brand-new kit bag – a tall, white, heavy tube of a thing. First in shoes, right at the bottom. Next go underclothes, then our many other belongings. Among the last our RAF shirt (will get *very* creased) and jacket (even more creased) and on top our tin hat. Pull up the rope and secure. Everybody ready? Don't forget your gas mask. Sling it over left shoulder. At last, READY!

Now what is it the men do? Hold rope at top, raise bag, swing it forward and it lands neatly on one shoulder. Easy!

OK girls. Ready? We nearly die laughing. Bags swing forward six inches

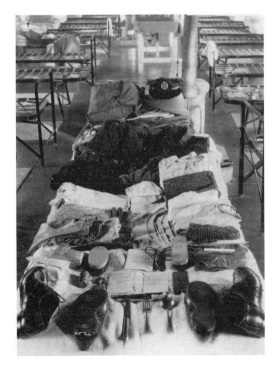

All this to go into one kit bag? Notice the beds in the background at High Ercall, 1942 (Jean Darling)

then drop back again with a heavy thud. Obviously we've got to get up a bit of strength. Try again. A bit better! Bags swing to waist height, then we all lurch forward with the bags as they land two feet ahead of us. Hm. Suppose we were to work up a swinging motion back and forth a couple of times and then up? OK. Try anything once – one, and two and three and UP! Chaos! Half of us get swung off our feet, and the rest nearly kill the WAAF next to us. Tin hats clatter out. It's no good! Hopeless!

Someone has a bright idea. What if we stood the bags up somewhere high and then just ease our shoulder under the bag. Sounds feasible. Look around hut – nowhere high! Well! Stand it on the bed and we could kneel down. Arms around kit bags and heave onto beds. Go down on knees. Success. I can't get up. Well! Push! Push! If I push any harder I'll have a baby. Stagger up. We're all standing tilted over at an angle of 45 degrees, with a kit bag between shoulder and neck. Daren't straighten up, or kit bag will roll off shoulder. Everybody ready?

Out of the hut! Careful how you go through that door. Twenty yards to the waiting lorry. Knees bent, body tilted, hat nearly falling off, gas mask swinging wildly. Made it! Drop kit bag from shoulder. What a relief. RAF drivers throw kit bags up on to lorry and then help us to clamber up. Think they quite enjoyed that. Bottoms up!

Drive to the railway station along country lanes singing, 'She'll Be Coming Round the Mountain When She Comes'. Quieten down when we reach the town and the station.

RAF drivers come to the back of the lorry, let down the tailboard and help us down. 'Hey. Careful where you put those hands!' Wolf whistles. We retrieve our kit bags, pull down our skirts, adjust jackets, push gas masks round the back. We all look at the kit bags and then each other. There's only one thing for it – we'll have to *drag* the wretched things! What a din . . . Whoever wrote that song, 'Pack Up Your Troubles in Your Old Kit Bag', got it wrong! It's the KIT BAG that's all the trouble!'

2
WHERE WE LIVED

The RAF had a great surprise! It did not expect WAAF until, at the very least, a few months *after* war broke out. Stations were therefore totally unprepared for their arrival, when, at the last moment, Air Ministry changed its mind!

As a result Jane Trefusis-Forbes, the WAAF Director – herself only appointed on 1 July 1939, slightly ahead of the Heads of the other women's services and just before most government departments closed for the summer holidays – was not able to produce the first Official WAAF Regulations until December 1939! RAF Stations had little enough accommodation for their men, let alone their women! As in the First World War, it was a typically scrambled start!

A hastily adopted, temporary expedient was to use Station Married Quarters, vacated by the families of airmen and Officers. When the war began, Joan Dann was first accommodated in one of these. 'In the lounge we had a cupboard on each side of the fireplace, which we hadn't opened until the first WAAF Commanding Officer's inspection. She opened the door and out tumbled dozens of empty beer bottles. The previous occupant had evidently been very fond of his ale!'

Joining as a Balloon Repairer at the end of October 1939, Eileen Jacobs considers that her first posting from Chigwell to Felixstowe might be amusing now, but it wasn't so at the time:

On our arrival on the station there was much panic. We were not expected. They had never had women before. No rations! Not on station strength! They opened up some damp and dreary Married Quarters, where we slept that night. Next day, not knowing what to do with us, they sent us off on twelve days leave over Xmas. We returned in January to find one foot of snow, still no issue greatcoats, and were issued instead with men's gum boots, dungarees and balaclavas. It was freezing working on the balloons in the sea-plane hangars right on the sea front!

Balloon Repairers in dungarees are grouped outside the Fabric Workers' hangar, Felixstowe, spring 1940 (Eileen Jacobs)

Another option was to lodge girls with local landladies in what were termed 'digs' or 'billets'.

At Hull, or rather Withersea, Pamela Anderson and two others found themselves billeted on a Mrs Dearing.

We slept in a double bed with a single mattress and one on an armchair and stool. Later we discovered that two prostitutes used the bed on a working day. A Naval Officer slept in the bath – the only place he could find. When asking the landlady where we washed, she replied, 'Well. It's not that you really need to wash, dear, is it? It's just that it freshens you up occasionally.' Mostly she gave us 1s 6d [quite generous then, but today equivalent to 15p] to buy lunch at the local NAAFI, but on one occasion the pet white rabbit of her ten-year-old son disappeared. We all knew what we were eating in the stew that night when her son kept asking where Robert the rabbit had gone.

Mrs Dearing and her son slept in a small indoor shelter, which served as our dining table, and after putting out our food with a large jar of pickles, she would retire with her son and his rabbit underneath, while we three WAAF ate our meal on top, to the accompaniment of her snores and our giggles.

Some billets didn't always work out, however, as Betty Trull reveals:

On my return from Bath to Blackpool very late at night, as I walked up the pathway to the house in the pouring rain and complete blackout, I kept falling over someone's belongings. Then I found that our landlady had thrown our things into the front garden and locked us out – about eight of us – because she wanted to take in civilian holiday-makers. We poor WAAF were out all night! We chummed up with some soldiers, who were also locked out, and we sat in a sea-front shelter all that night. Next day, when our WAAF Admin Officer got to hear of it, there was a flap!

Many buildings were simply taken over by the services. Living in some requisitioned houses in Gosport, Newcastle, Mavis Pickford remembers the terrible winter of 1940:

the worst for many years. Life could be a bit grim without heating and hot water – this was considered an unnecessary luxury in those days, except for a bath, usually once a week. Regulations decreed that all personnel must sleep in a room with an open window, so we took turns – dressed for bed as though going on an Arctic expedition – to be the one to open the French windows

Meads Lodge – a requisitioned house in Newcastle, February, 1941. 'We lived here, with meals in another, through the whole of that awful winter.' Note the white French doors, which were opened at night! (Mavis Pickford)

and then make a quick retreat into bed. The hot water problem was solved by a few enterprising girls getting the kitchen range going. We never asked where the fuel came from, but the fence between the houses gradually disappeared!

At Leighton Buzzard in 1941 Valerie Allingham was 'living in the Old Workhouse. While we were there, one girl lost her false teeth down the toilet. Then she had to explain and draw a diagram of where and how she lost them.'

At another posting Marjorie Then was billeted in an ex-private boys' school. 'In the bathroom all the baths and basins were in a row with no dividers. At first there was consternation on the part of the shy. Later, when curtains were put up, there was more consternation – everyone had enjoyed the morning wash and gossip sessions!'

Streets, vehicles and buildings in Britain were blacked out to give no light which might act as guidance to enemy planes. Everywhere they went the airwomen were exhorted to economize and Phyllis Smart complains bitterly about one idea:

> They took our too-bright lights away,
> And gave us bulbs of blue
> Which really made our billets look
> An awful ghastly hue.
> We cannot see to wash or clean,
> It really is too much,
> Taking a bath, we must rely
> Purely on sense of touch.

Living in a London hostel at Vincent Square, Joan Raine one evening,

started to run a bath. I left it for a minute, went to my room and stopped to natter to some some friends there. Meanwhile the bath water was cascading down into the well of the building. Suddenly a Sergeant appeared at the door of my room very irate, demanding to know who was running a bath. I agreed it was me and was put on a charge, 'for having more than five inches of water in my bath'. I got a reprimand; I also, never forgot the bath tap in future.

Another London hostel-dweller, Evelyn Whalley, remembers the day

we were queuing for our chocolate ration, and the dear WVS lady, who ran the hostel, came up and said, 'How many baths have you had this week?' To us, being northerners, it sounded like bars. So, thinking she was talking about chocolate bars, we said, 'Oh. We don't bother if we never have any!' I, in turn, said, 'Sometimes if I have been on leave, I have two at once – it doesn't bother me going without altogether.' Seeing the horrified look on the poor lady's face, we suddenly realized what she had meant. 'Oh. You mean *baths*!', we chorused. The poor lady retreated, and I'm sure she thought we were taking the mickey!

In some extremely large buildings, poor past-maintenance often resulted in rooms being damp. Irrespective of this, once settled comfortably, girls fought against further upheaval. This plaintive plea from the three occupants was pinned to the door of their condemned room for the Inspecting Medical Officer:

> We blacked the grate, we stained the floor,
> We even dusted the top of the door.
> We pinched the curb, we swiped the chair,
> We swept the floor with the utmost care.
> So if our room we have to quit,
> And to the huts are made to flit,

Culzean Park, a requisitioned property. The Recreation Room was 'a grim place, no carpeting, little warmth,' March 1941 (Mavis Pickford)

> In case a little damp is proved,
> For fear of having to be moved,
> We write this verse and tend this plea,
> And trust we'll get some sympathy.
> It will be to our greatest sorrow,
> To have to move upon the morrow,
> So, although a line we do not shoot,
> We hope we will not GET THE BOOT.

The plea was unsuccessful, but the tenacious three stayed together in another room in a different building!

Stately homes made ideal billets, but their size could sometimes cause misunderstandings. At Exton Hall Corporal Joyce Stevenson (an NCO) was escorting a WAAF Officer on an Inspection. 'Some shift workers were always there sleeping. As I opened the door of one of the eight bathrooms, we stopped dead on seeing a girl seated on a lavatory. Her training did not desert her. You stood up when an Officer came into the room. So she did, with her knickers draped around her ankles.'

Nissen huts, with their corrugated metal covering, were evident on most stations. They were not popular for sleeping accommodation, being poorly insulated; their only means of heating was usually a black, pot-bellied, floor-fixed stove – one per hut – made of cast-iron that had to be blackleaded daily. It had a large pipe as flue and a voracious appetite for fuel.

Doreen May's hut was near a farm and one night a cow got stuck in the entrance. 'I also remember positioning myself in line, so that I would draw the bed in the centre near the stove.'

Christine Watson noted another unsuspected feature of the huts: 'I remember being woken up in the small hours by New Forest ponies kicking the blazes out of our Nissen hut. It appeared they liked the sound! They also liked galloping up and down the runways and we had a yellow-painted jeep (the "Yellow Peril") especially for chasing them away, so that the planes could take off.' The most often encountered criticism is voiced by Kathleen Watts. 'Our Nissen huts were not only shaped like igloos but they mostly felt as cold.' Her opinion is shared by Mary Ward. 'Our Nissen hut accommodation and the ablutions on wartime camps were spartan! Especially in winter when there was mud or snow or ice around. One had to be heroic to go for a wash, let alone a bath!'

Possibly the best kind of huts were those of timber or concrete in garden-shed style. Sometimes they contained more than one room, with a separate one (bunk)

Ready for bed, outside Nissen Hut 6 at Hinxton Hall in July 1942. Note the newly issued service striped pyjamas, tin hats, cocoa mugs, hot water bottle and cigarette (Zillah Driver)

for an NCO. Very rarely were the ablutions tacked onto one end, as their proximity was deemed unhealthy. When, later on in the war, some girls were lucky enough to move into brick-built barrack blocks on camp, it was 'like moving into Buckingham Palace' – the verdict of one delighted girl.

For most airwomen, however, accommodation was mainly in huts of one kind or another. In some hurriedly erected huts at St David's Head, Sylvia Swinburne lost hundreds of bed sheets, 'presumably because airwomen were sorry for the airmen, who had no sheets, and supplied their boyfriends with them.'

Life in winter was a constant struggle against the cold, and reaching the far-distant ablution blocks. 'Who will ever forget those freezing bath houses?' asks Joyce Stevenson, 'with the black line on the bath tub four inches up, and the wooden duck boards? In winter, it was an act of courage to have a bath. Some didn't!' On the other hand, outside Welton near Scampton, Joan Pearce had mixed feelings when she was 'trudging along to have a bath, over crisp white virgin snow under a brilliant full moon, clad only in pyjamas and greatcoat.'

At one time when the WAAF bath hut was out of order (U/S), Irene Poole and a friend 'took a chance and shared a bath in the men's bath hut, which when we entered was unoccupied. However, an airman came in later and took the other bath, and with the snorts and grunts he was making, we could hardly control our giggles. Nevertheless, we managed to escape unseen.' Dorothy Neenan recalls 'coming back from a weekend pass to find the pipes frozen. So there were thirty of us washing in one small red fire-bucket. Our comment, "If our mothers could only see us now!"' In a similar situation, Margaret Furness remembers

being without any fuel whatever in the winter of 1944, and having to break the ice on your tin bowl to get some sort of a wash. Wooden chairs and clothes-horses (via the Officers' Batwomen) were secretly chopped up to burn in the stoves. Carpenters (chippies) were ardently wooed to coax wood out of them. They turned up on dates with a bundle of wood, rather than the usual bunch of roses or box of Black Magic chocolates!

At the other extreme, while billeted in huts on a golf course at Northwood, Gwendoline Whipps recalls: 'On one very hot night, we decided to sleep outside. Unknown to us, sheep had been put to graze on the course and during the night they decided to investigate us. We awoke to find ourselves overrun by sheep.' 'Our accommodation and food was certainly very adequate,' remarks Barbara Hughes, 'except when the coal man came and dumped the coal in the bin at the bottom of my bed in our hut, while I was out on night duty.' One day was enlivened for Lily Yates' hut at Hednesford where,

it was customary to leave a mug of cocoa warming on the stove and make the bed of anyone coming back on a weekend pass. On Sunday this had been done and next morning we called Joan, a known sleepy-head, to get up. Instead, a man surfaced from her place. With a shriek we all leapt back into bed until he had left. Later he returned to apologize, via our hut Corporal. Apparently his bed was in the same position as Joan's, and as luck would have it, she had missed her train connection.

Disaster struck at Chicksands for Sheila Parker, when 'the Corporal in charge of our hut was Rosemary Portal, daughter of the British Chief of Air Staff. She dried off a towel in front of the fire, went out, it caught alight and the hut was burned down, including an airwoman's wedding dress. We held dances and scrounged coupons from home to replace items lost.'

Stations often moved personnel from hut to hut at a moment's notice, as Alma Jones describes:

> The raucous sound of the Tannoy loudspeaker system shattered my dreams, dragging me from a deep sleep after a night watch as Plotter. The voice repeated, 'Number 4 Watch, changing quarters. The lorry outside will wait 5 minutes to take your kit. Anything not on the lorry must be carried.' It took a couple of minutes before the meaning penetrated my brain. Staggering out of bed, I stuffed everything into my kit bag, threw it on the lorry and collapsed into the comfort of my bed. Wait a minute! I had put *everything* (bath towel, toilet bag, uniforms, shoes) on the lorry and had only the pyjamas I was wearing. Oh no! 'Hang on! Stop! Stop!'

Food also caused complaints from many airwomen. On a Gas course Marjorie Bradford remembers, 'We had our meals by candlelight in a condemned hangar. The food was all on one plate – stew on one side and prunes and custard on the other.'

Eva Cormacey spent most of her service years in the Records Office at Gloucester. There,

> the food was dreadful. We were often served liver, which looked green, out of galvanized buckets for breakfast. We put it straight into the pig bin. [Vegetables were everywhere overcooked, together with the old faithful cabbage, nicknamed 'Shredded Gas Capes' according to Phyllis O'Neil!] At tea, we would find large soup plates full of jam and treacle on our trestle tables, and they would be covered with wasps. We would fish out the wasps and line them up, all along the tables!
>
> It was a very special treat when eggs were on the menu! We had a runner, who took draft notes to other departments, and she would enquire at the Cookhouse on her way back. If eggs were there, she would rush into the office and shout, 'Eggs for tea', and as soon as the signal was given to cease work there was a mad rush to the Cookhouse, everyone coming from all departments.

Girls learned not to criticize their food, as Elizabeth Zegveldt found, when for a dare she complained about the eyes in the potatoes 'to the Orderly Officer, who asked, "Any complaints?" as usual at our supper. As a result I ended the rest of my

Helping out with the spud bashing, High Street, 1943. The Cookhouse is in the background (Pat Evans)

evening – four hours – sitting in the kitchen, digging the eyes out of the potatoes!'
An airwoman with fewer complaints was Daphne Donnelly who, however,

found I could not survive on what was served up on Breakfast Parade at 7.45, when we queued in the dining room after the right tune came from the Tannoy. So I got there early, scoffed what only seemed like an appetizer, went outside to wash my utensils, and returned to the end of the queue for some more. However, the cooks quickly cottoned on to this and told me to wait, and there was always some over for me!

While I was away one weekend on a 48-hour pass, some of the girls eating in the Mess were poisoned, because the cooks had put stewed apple into lead bowls!'

Drivers like Betty Haywood often went hungry, 'missing many meals because of our conditions of work. I well remember one dark, wet night at Castle Donnington, when two of us tried to milk a cow, armed only with a torch and a cocoa tin. We were not successful, I'm afraid, and had to drink milkless cocoa that night.'

The airwomen's accommodation, complete with its own Guardroom, was usually separated from the rest of the camp and out of bounds to airmen. One evening Mabel Payne had to cancel a date with her fiancé

because the Corporal on duty in the Guardroom was ill and I was replacing her. Peter was disappointed but said 'Cheerio. See you at 2300 hours' (the time WAAF had to be in, and much resented as airmen were free till 2400). I laughed and said, 'See you in the morning.'

However, at eleven o'clock prompt, in walked Peter, unusually drunk. I was horrified. I tried to get him out of the door, but he kept giggling. Then I saw the Duty Officer and Sergeant approaching, so I pushed him into the room next door, where the Duty Airwoman was sleeping. The young WAAF Officer checked the records, asking me if everything was OK, as I must have looked flustered. Then I heard a couple of chuckles coming from next door. As the Officer went out, she gave me a broad grin and a wink. Goodness knows what she thought. I gave them a few minutes to go, after which I got Peter safely off forbidden territory.

In those days, with little radio and no television, there was more time for talk during leisure hours. Warnings of spies and German parachutists were constantly in the minds of airwomen. 'At Gatcombe Park, where we WAAF were billeted (now the country house of Princess Anne, who, I notice, was complaining of mice, as we had done)', says Dilys Upton, 'it was a long walk back in the dark. One late evening I was startled by a huge form, which suddenly rose up just in front of me. I felt my knees begin to buckle, but then I saw that the huge form was two cart-horses. They were probably as scared as I was.' 'You have no idea how dark is dark,' comments Doreen May, 'unless you have experienced a night with no moon, a heavy fog and in World War II's blackout.'

At a ghost-talking session, Mavis Pickford remembers that

someone said the ghost of Lady Hillingdon was sometimes seen haunting the stream through the camp. Next morning before daylight, I was walking across the little bridge, when I saw what looked like something white bobbing about above the stream. I was petrified. However, as the apparition neared, I realized it was an airman with a white towel around his neck going for a bath.

Another nerve-racking incident came Vera Blackwell's way:

When I was stationed at Westend, Southampton, we lived in a large requisitioned house. The top part of the house was unsafe after being bombed, and so was unoccupied. One night I was awakened by our Sergeant – she was a quite large girl and I was the smallest WAAF in the house. She said she had heard a noise up in the empty rooms, and as the house was supposed to be haunted, she didn't want to go up there on her own. So, half-asleep, I found myself going up the stairs on my own, with the Sergeant at the foot, holding the torch. When I reached the room, I could hear a flapping sound, so I opened the door carefully. The noise had been made by a large piece of wallpaper, hanging off the wall and caught by the wind from a broken window. When the Sergeant was told, she asked me not to tell the other girls that she had sent me up there.

More scary was the tale told by Margaret Wilson:

I was billeted in a big house that had belonged to a Major, about a mile from the camp at Chippenham. It had hidden passages and a big stone-flagged hall. We had to take turns to light the fire in the beautiful old fireplace. However, I had been told that the place was haunted.

One night I started to light the fire, but felt that there was someone watching me, so I kept turning round. All of a sudden someone said, 'Do you like it here?' I froze. It turned out to be the owner of the house. I was eventually brought back to consciousness and we had a good laugh! The owls used to glare at us through the windows and if we knocked a wooden panel, it would spring open and reveal steps to the cellar. We were told that Oliver Cromwell had once stayed here. He was welcome!

There are two *real* ghost stories, however, in which airwomen were concerned. The first involved Vida Grieve who was billeted, with nine other WAAF, in a hostel in Weyhill Road, Andover, and slept in the library.

Almost every evening after lights out, the door would open and there was the sound of footsteps walking over the floor. A few minutes later the footsteps retreated and the door closed, just as if someone had come to choose a book from the library shelf. When the lights went on, there was no one there. At other nights, a grandfather clock chimed the hours, but there was no grandfather clock in the house! Additionally the backstairs and passages always had an eerie feel about them.

The second one took place at Dishforth at the end of the war, where Margaret Jones was billeted in ex-RAF Quarters where they had a room each.

In my room, I remember, on one or two nights, I could swear there was a cat, pressing its paws up and down my bed from top to bottom. When the lights were on there was nothing there and no one could get into my room. It happened several times. Maybe it was the ghost of an airman sleeping in my room, who had been killed. It was frightening and strange!

In a similar vein, Joan Osborne-Walker was reported to have been killed with three others at Coltishall on 26 April 1941. 'I was on leave at the time, and on returning to camp I met an airman, who literally turned a sickly shade of greeny-white on seeing me, as he thought I was a ghost.'

3
OUR DAYS ON CAMP

Despite the manifold disadvantages of daily life on camp, the comradeship enjoyed by the airwomen – maybe as fellow-sufferers in misfortune – more than made up for the drawbacks. 'The years that I spent in the WAAF', considers Josephine Goldie-Scot, 'were a valuable and happy experience for which I shall always be grateful. I appreciated the friendship and kindness of colleagues, especially as I was very innocent and naïve when I joined. I remember in particular a loose-living former usherette with a heart of gold, who took it upon herself to protect me from the more worldly elements and wouldn't let anyone swear in my presence. As I'd already been in the WAAF for six months by then, I was amused but none the less appreciative.'

Such friendships were built from many things. For instance Primrose Skinner 'asked a young cockney WAAF mechanic to join our group. After introducing ourselves, she looked up at me – she was about 5 ft or less and I am 5 ft 11 in – and said, "What's your name again?" I looked down at her and said, "Primrose, but they call me Prim for short." "Blimey," she replied, "they ought to have called you 'Olly 'Ock!"

Airwomen could also cry and laugh together, with great emphasis on the latter. In Joyce Meeks' hut was 'an airwoman who was double-jointed. She used to sit in bed with her feet and legs encased in a pair of aircrew long-socks behind her shoulders and talk to her feet, waggling them in reply.'

One special virtue was the 'all for one and one for all' attitude, as Beatrice Rigby exemplifies. She was the Corporal in charge of a hut of twenty-eight airwomen.

After a dance in our barrack room, we had a lot of sandwiches, fruit cake and lemonade over, which were put in a cardboard box under my bed until the midnight visit of the Duty WAAF Officer was over. So when it got to 12.30 p.m., we decided she mustn't be coming and we would have a bean feast. Everyone was crowded around my bed when we heard our outer door open. All the girls flew back to their beds pretending sleep, but, of course, I was caught, sitting up in bed clutching this huge cardboard box. When the WAAF Officer looked at me, I said sweetly, 'Parcel from Home, Ma'am'. She knew, but answered just as sweetly, 'Carry on Corporal!' and left. Afterwards we giggled and tucked in.

Another night's entertainment, fortunately only rarely tried, is described by Alma Jones.

One night, the girls decided to try spirit writing, each with a finger and thumb on the pencil. But the pencil would not move. Then I was persuaded to join in and suddenly the pencil moved and careered all over the paper. When we looked, there was a large, crudely-drawn picture of a gun. Then triangles were drawn all round it.

'Was this a warning?' we asked. 'Why don't you write?'

The pencil drew a left hand.

'Who are you?' we enquired.

A daisy-like flower was drawn. But it wasn't a daisy!

We drew a figure and said, 'If you're a WAAF add buttons.'

Buttons were added.

'Where are you?' we asked.

The pencil drew a spiral.

Down the hole we guessed (our Ops Room of No. 11 Fighter Group was deep underground).

Then we realized – Rita – short for Margarita. She had been shot, accidentally, through her right hand and chest as we Plotters came off duty, and we had given her a military funeral! There came a change and the pencil started writing, but the only sensible thing I remember was Hilda asking, 'Where is my vest?'

The pencil wrote, 'Under your bed.'

She looked and there it was. I promise you this is true!

There was often a love-hate relationship between airwomen and their stations, as typified in this poem by Phyllis Smart (with apologies to Robert Browning):

> Oh to be in Wallop, now that winter's here,
> And whoever wakes in Wallop, sees some morning, unaware
> That the cinder path and the asphalt road
> To a depth of feet is completely snowed,

And we curse the place as we homeward plough,
In Wallop now!
And after winter, when spring follows,
And through the mud the poor WAAF wallows,
And water drips from the leaking eaves
And colds and flu spring up in sheaves,
Then the mud is dried and the white chalk flies,
Far worse than Hitler's gasses in our eyes!

Most girls could understand the tragedy clouding their relationships and took both in their stride, realizing that the RAF wanted them only in order to release its men for first-line duties. 'Many men missed their wives and seemed to think there would be no tomorrow', writes Margaret Rayworth. 'Sad really! Had I not seen what those men – some only boys – did against all odds, I would have found those years the most wonderful of my life. Friendship! Help! If you were late, girls would put their pillows in your bed before the Duty Officer came round.'

Articles of uniform, also, came in for much good-natured and affectionate ridicule. In a sexually reticent era, WAAF slang gave knickers many names:

Prize-winning WAAF Twilights in
1945–6 (Joy Bishop)

'blackouts' for winter, 'twilights' for summer, and Janet Knox's favourite, 'Harvest Festivals', because 'all was safely gathered in'. Not so amusing was taking these items back to the Clothing Store, 'on our Clothing Exchange Parade, when', according to Kathleen Wilkie, 'the RAF Personnel used to embarrass the poor airwomen by holding them up and saying, "Is this fair wear and tear?"' 'I remember', Margaret Rayworth continues, 'during Kit Inspection in our hut, one airwoman had lost her blackouts. When the Officer inspected everything went well. The only thing was that two of our WAAF were not wearing any knickers at all!'

An uncommon feature of uniform was pointed out by Jacqueline Bragg. 'I was always attached to Fighter Command, and so we used to walk about with the top button of our tunic undone, which was supposed to be the correct thing to do.' (In fact, they were copying the pilots.)

There was the Daily Inspection (DI) of the special bed pack, which was made up, according to rule, of pillows, blankets, sheets and mattresses [known as biscuits]. There were also Domestic Nights, which came round once a week, forcing all the airwomen to stay in and do 'housework' all evening. It was bitterly resented because airmen escaped it. Nevertheless it did have its compensations, for on this night, as Edith Clist discovered, 'room mates became friends. You told one another little secrets, you told of broken dates, broken hearts and swore life-long friendships.' She incidentally commented that airwomen considered 'Senior NCOs too bossy and Officers to be respected and avoided.' In her diary Phyllis Gittins notes one Domestic Night:

Polished round my bed space. The lino has come up in big bubbles, and now the bubbles have burst, we cheerfully polish round the holes. We all have a good laugh – we find plenty to laugh about, regardless! Made our toast and cocoa, spread the pickles and cheese around (a gift from home). Good old Mum! Enjoyed the warmth and companionship. Bed about 10.30.

Edith Clist describes another Domestic Night:

In our hut, about a dozen WAAF, dressed only in bra and blackouts, began dancing a tango. It was the funniest sight! An Officer looked in and was doubled up with laughter. What made it funnier was that everybody stopped dead, when they realized there was an Officer present. Then it was a rush to 'stand by your beds'. What a sight. All those blackouts standing to attention!

Cleaning duty, Broughton House, 96 Group, 1942 (Joyce Williams)

On Domestic Nights too, articles such as sheets, towels and collars, were changed for laundry. On one occasion a friend collected Dilys Upton's clean laundry for her while she was on leave. 'When I returned there were two items missing and *I* was put on a charge for losing them!'

Mary Doole wrote:

> Joyful little ladies, clad in Air Force Blue;
> Buttons all a-shining, souls a-shining, too.
>
> Sometimes we're unhappy, sometimes we are sad;
> But whatever our emotions, we're seldom very bad.
>
> Oh! You ought to see us, standing in the rain,
> Telling dear old David to send it down again.

But what is most pathetic — a sight to bring a tear,
Make honest men have pity; dishonest shake with fear,

To see a lonely little WAAF, with bundle small and white,
Slowly treading weary steps, before the ending night.

But those who may have evil thoughts a-buzzing in their brain,
It's not what you're a-thinking of — but laundry! Fooled again!

Another bit of WAAF jargon is recalled by Gladys Carter, a Belgian escapee. 'Anything we couldn't think of straightaway was called a "Doefer". For example, "put it on the doefer", or "going to the doefer". Everything was a doefer!'

After 'Lights Out' curious things could sometimes happen, according to Nita Goldsmith. 'Cold cream was sold in tins, as was shoe-polish blacking. One night, in the dark, an airwoman spread blacking on her face, thinking it was face cream!'

Though there was plenty of public transport in those days, it was often far from camps, and petrol restrictions eliminated most cars. Thus bicycles became a prized and necessary possession. However, 'when I arrived at Bradwell, I couldn't ride a bicycle,' discloses Joyce Chadwell, 'so it was up to me to learn fast. One day, on a supposedly unused runway, I was wobbling along, barely keeping my balance, when

On my bike! Cranwell, 1942 (Phyllis Moore)

to my horror, a plane landed behind me. I thought if I turned into a hangar the plane would go by, but it didn't! *It* turned in too, and I was petrified! The pilot jumped out grinning all over his face and thought it a huge joke. But in those few minutes, I really learned to ride a bike!'

On another occasion Eva Cormacey was putting her bicycle away in the shed, 'when I saw a man in uniform approaching. Do I salute or not? His uniform was strange to me. To be on the safe side I hid behind the shed until he had passed. The outcome was that he was an airman, sent out dressed as a German Officer, to test our alert state!'

Service writing dictated a form of Official report which sometimes had peculiar results, as when Joyce Barnes notified her Commanding Officer, 'Sir, I have the honour to state that my bicycle, no. SN/301 has been stolen . . .'

A much valued concession was an occasional flight in an aircraft. Taking an Air Ambulance course at Hendon, Louie McGaughey and those with her 'were to be taken for a 15 minute flight in an Anson. The first group landed and then the rest of us scrambled aboard. We were very excited, and as we started to descend we said we were sorry we could not go on longer. Suddenly the pilot started to go up again, and flew us round for another 15 minutes. When we landed one of the girls turned to the pilot and thanked him for such a long flight. He replied, 'Don't thank me. The undercarriage was jammed, so I couldn't land!'

After an explosion at RAF Fauld, Lily Yates and some WAAF 'went to assist from Tattenhill. There had been many deaths and we saw chickens plucked clean as whistles and cattle lying as if made of stone. So, for about a week, there was just the air party on camp. When we did eventually fly, I had the pilot's cat on my knee, and it was sick at both ends. The pilot thought it a huge joke!'

A sad incident is mentioned by Doreen Strickland in her letter home from Inverness at the end of June 1941.

Our WAAF Mess Corporal, who was very popular, has died and her father was very anxious she should be given a military funeral. We had to do the slow march all the way from the main square to the cemetery on the hill. The Adjutant, who had meningitis as a child, was a bit unsteady, and the Air Vice Marshal had an artificial leg, so I found being marker a bit tricky, as the Parade tended to sway! Buglers from the Cameron Highlanders sounded the last post and it was quite a moving experience.

There were, of course, medical problems specific to WAAF, such as pregnancy, which was a terrible disgrace and a real tragedy for unmarried girls in those days. The Corporals (NCOs) working for Sylvia Swinburne, when she became a WAAF G Officer, had instructions that 'any airwoman who could not do up the third button of her tunic, was to be sent to me. On one occasion, a fat cook was marched into my office. She said, "I know what you are going to say, Ma'am, but it isn't. It's me corsets!"'

Peggy Westwood, as an Administrative Sergeant, had a long chat with one of her cooks, who *was* pregnant, 'about her future and if the father was likely to marry her. After a time she named an airman and asked me to talk to him. When faced with the problem he said, "Well. It's like this Sarge. I'm just a shareholder in a very large company!"'

Ordinarily, medical arrangements were not always as private as Joyce Curtis liked. 'I didn't like the queuing, although it was surprising to see airwomen flirting while waiting for jabs. We all used to have our sleeves rolled up and hands on hips waiting. Lambs to the slaughter!'

On many stations male and female doctors treated airmen and airwomen in the same surgeries. Betty Ingle tells of one occasion, 'when having an Overseas Medical at Cosford, I had stripped. The Medical Officer rang for a nurse and in walked an airman. "Bloody Hell," cried the Medical Officer. "I must have pressed the wrong button!"'

Sore eyes sent Nora Daniels to Station Sick Quarters. 'The Medical Officer [MO] gave me a chit to take to the Dispenser who, lifting a large jar from the shelf,

'One girl fainted before the needle touched her' (specially drawn by David Langdon from 1941 original)

poured some into a glass, added water and handed it to me saying, "Here. Drink this and come back this afternoon." A fellow WAAF whom she told, laughed. "Silly girl. You drank your eye-bath!" Well, it seemed to do the trick anyway.'

'One of the nicest things about service life', says Pat Sparks,

> was the number of people one met. We had girls from Eire, Canada, Uruguay, South Africa, America, Australia and a New Zealand Officer.
> On my first station one of the girls near me caught scarlet fever. We were all sent to Sick Bay for a check up by the MO. He was a young Canadian and asked me if I smoked. Nervously I admitted that I did, thinking he would tell me to stop. Instead he said, 'Have you a match? I haven't had a cigarette all day!'

Not liking her present work, Jessie White

> decided to remuster to the trade of Maps and Charts (which automatically carried a Corporal's stripes.) My WAAF Officer told me that the only way

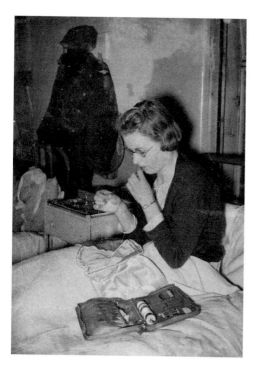

Hospitalized at Uxbridge in March 1941. Note the 'hussif' in use (Jean Darling)

would be on Medical grounds. But how was·I, a very healthy and fit-looking WAAF going to do so?

Eventually I reported to the MO, who was not at all keen to do anything for me because 'It would mean me writing a report as long as my arm'. I stood my ground and he gave me one or two tests and then said he would check my hearing. He covered one of my ears and then stood away from me and whispered words. When he said 'solicitor' I said 'sister', and for 'glancing' I said 'dancing', etc. I think he probably knew what I was doing, and I can't think now how I dared to do it! My determination paid off, and I shortly started training for Maps and Charts!

The Examination Papers of Medical Orderlies could produce some howlers, like, 'In giving artificial respiration, never give up hope until the doctor arrives', and 'a suppository is the place where furniture is stored'.

At Mildenhall Beryl Seal-Morgan, with others, played a trick on their Junior Medical Officer. 'We put his small sports car in his surgery with a record sheet on its bonnet, giving its symptoms and faults and asked for treatment. He reported his prize possession as stolen until he entered his surgery and found it.'

Another amusing story comes from Jeanne Williams:

I reported to Sick Quarters in January 1942, at the top of the Royal Hotel, Inverness, with mumps and was to be sent to hospital. I was cocooned in army blankets and strapped on to a stretcher. As they had to carry me down the numerous stairs, the journey was hair-raising. But then the airmen stretcher-bearers tried to take me through the hotel revolving doors! When we finally got outside (by another door) the ambulance had not arrived. So the airmen put the stretcher on the kerb of the High Street, with my small kit at my feet and my cap on my chest. The Inverness people being very respectful, the women bowed their heads and the men removed their hats as they passed me! Eventually the ambulance arrived and I was allowed to return to the land of the living!

Dental Orderlies, working with the camp dentist (when such was available), were given a thorough training, which enabled Daphne Cole to observe, mischievously, 'There was an outbreak of gingivitis on camp. Apparently bleeding gums can be caused by drinking utensils and kissing. If that is so, the whole camp will have to be treated!' 'I had dental treatment at Stafford', affirms Elizabeth

Dental Hygienists skipping at Sidmouth, 1943 (Vera Scott)

Taverner, another WAAF, 'and the name of the dentist was Flight Lieutenant Fillingham! It doesn't sound true but it is!'

To bring them to emergency war readiness, stations regularly held various kinds of drills and exercises. Since gas had been used by the enemy in the First World War, the whole population of Britain, as a precaution in the Second World War, had been issued with gas masks which had to be carried everywhere. Unfortunately for WAAF, with no handbags and the filling of pockets strictly forbidden, Margaret Laing admits that

> airwomen were in the habit of filling the respirator box with articles we needed for the day or weekend, e.g. face cream, powder, hair curlers etc. One weekend my respirator became mixed with a soldier's. We had Gas Drill the next week and I wasn't too keen on wearing his respirator, nor, I expect, did he mine (as well as the contents falling out!) I don't know who was the most embarrassed. Later we re-exchanged them.

One friend of Monica Hughes 'always used to carry her breakfast marmalade in her respirator case, until we were unexpectedly called on Parade one morning after breakfast. In her hurry she did not put the lid on firmly and this sticky mess oozed down her skirt!'

At High Ercoll, Doreen Burd was put in charge of the Gas Cleansing Centre for weekly anti-gas exercises. 'For this I had to get into full kit of gas mask, long stiff cape, tin hat, boots etc., "looking like a bloody Christmas Tree", as my Squadron Leader said.' While Betty Ingle thought 'we looked like pregnant elephants'.

During Gas Drill, Vera Homer was always 'stationed at the door, asking "Have you seen to the wants of nature?" as the girls filed into the Gas Room. We always fell about laughing.'

Even when well organized, things did not always go according to plan. As a runner on a Gas Exercise at Compton Basset, Gwendoline Scase was 'fully kitted out with heavy gas equipment, mask and wellington boots, several sizes too large. Unfortunately when the all-clear siren went, they forgot to dismiss the four wing runners – and running back and fore in a heatwave, with boots I could hardly raise off the ground, was an experience I'll never forget!'

Gas mask practice at Blackpool, December 1942 (Rene Cawson)

In another exercise Margaret Collinge was supposed to be a casualty. 'Fully dressed in my No. 5 Anti-Gas equipment, complete with label stating I was gassed but not wounded, I hid in the Mess as instructed. I stayed for half-an-hour and no one came. So I strolled outside and lay on the grass. Still no one discovered me. Finally, in desperation, I gave up and went to the Decontamination Centre myself.'

One Commanding Officer on Vera Homer's station 'thought we should also do fire fighting. None of us could hold the hose for a start, and when the water was turned on, we all fell down. It was cancelled soon afterwards!'

On the station where Eva Cormacey worked, 'a Warrant Officer put a match to the long grass on the camp to test whether the fire piquet was on the alert. The fire got out of control and the Gloucester Fire Brigade was sent for!'

A big security purge was set up at Fazackerly while Irene Wright and her friend were away.

As we returned, chatting away, suddenly out of the blackness of the night this voice boomed, 'Halt! Who goes there?' I stopped dead, speechless, but

March past the barrack hut, which was used as the Gas Decontamination Centre. There were 3,000 airwomen on the third WAAF Birthday Parade at Innsworth, June 1942 (Lesley Nightingale)

Nancy called out, 'It's all right! It's only us!' We never lived this down. Whenever we walked into the NAAFI or dining room, the boys would call, 'Here they are – the only two WAAF in the Air Force.'

Something similar happened to Elizabeth Walker:

Three friends and I, returning on a late pass, had borrowed a hurricane lantern from an Army Depot, where they had not refilled it. It went out, but we found our way back somehow. Arriving late we were challenged, 'Who goes there?', and I answered, 'Four Foolish Virgins!' As a result I was put on a charge and got ten days jankers [extra duties as punishment].

Daphne Richardson tells an amusing story about her dog:

I was allowed to keep it, provided he was registered and given his own number to prevent him being rounded up and taken away.

Wimpy (short for Wellington bomber) was a tiny little puppy sitting among broken glass in a bombed Portsmouth pet shop, so I took him back to Gosport Camp. Wimpy thrived. The funny thing was that his ears turned out to be just like wings!

A year later the Fleet Air Arm took over Gosport and I was posted to Swinderby and not allowed to take him with me, so I left him in charge of the Navy. Three weeks later I returned to Gosport to fetch him. Unfortunately the Navy was eating, all 500 of them! So I stood at the door and called him. With one bound from over the other side, Wimpy jumped up on the nearest table, and came across all the other tables, jumping across dinners and people. Fortunately, the Navy took it in good part and gave us a rousing cheer as I beat a hasty retreat with Wimpy.

He also got me into trouble one day when I was on duty. Wimpy should have been in the Boiler Room, but had been let in by one of the girls and was sitting on my bed. A WAAF Officer, taking Kit Inspection, tried to push him off the bed. The girls told me afterwards that it was worth *me* getting fourteen days Confined to Barracks [CB], just to see the Officer being chased down the middle of the hut!

Another unusual charge appeared when Joan Norman and friends, 'after a hectic night on watch, took our biscuits [mattresses] into the garden, as it was a beautiful day at Coltishall. We woke up at 2 p.m., badly sunburned and were put on a charge of "Wilful Neglect", and had three days CB.'

The Orderly Room was the name given to the hearing of an airwoman's misdemeanours by her Officer. This happened to Shelagh Pinchbeck, who with two friends was on a charge for a minor offence:

Our WAAF Officer's office was very small and the three of us standing in front of her desk almost reached from wall to wall. She gave us a little pep talk and then dismissed us. We came to attention and saluted – the only trouble was that the girl nearest the right wall was also nearest a set of shelves, and as she brought her arm up it connected with them and everything went all over the place! We were lucky the Officer had a sense of humour, and we did not find ourselves on a second charge of wrecking her Office!

Senior NCOs and Officers, too, could make mistakes. Closing down a station and dispersing 420 airwomen to various postings, Marjorie Bradford, now a Sergeant, 'worked through three days and two nights without sleep. In the turmoil, I forgot to cancel the 50 gallons of fresh milk, which were delivered daily – and there were only seven of us remaining!'

On another memorable occasion, while Doreen Burd was Night Duty Operations Officer at Headquarters Transport Command:

the Duty Traffic Office had made several 'hoax' phone calls to me (quickly revealed, so that no harm was done). Some time later a voice announced, 'This is SASO, Fighter Command', and I replied, 'And this is the Queen of Sheba!' To my horror it really *was* SASO, but he mercifully accepted my stumbling apologies, saw the joke and laughed loudly, before we got down to the business of a special fighter escort. At least he couldn't see my red face!

In 1944, when she became a Squadron Officer, Emmie Hawkins had to carry out regular nights of Duty Officer, and sleep in the (men's) RAF Officers' Mess. 'The following morning when the Batman came to call me, I asked him (wickedly) if he was the usual one on duty? "Oh no, Ma'am", he replied. "The usual Batman isn't married, so he wasn't considered suitable to call you. I am!"' This was while the RAF was still coming to terms with female Senior Officers!

4
ON THE MOVE

Drills and Parades, though not the airwomen's favourite occupation on camp, could not always be avoided, as many tried, but they were not so frequent as is sometimes believed. They had merits – apart from exercise in the open air – since they brought together girls who might never see one another because their living accommodation and work took them to far-flung areas of the camp. They were also expected to march and parade in the same way as the men, and along with them, though in separate flights. Nevertheless, shift work and priority trades often prevented girls and men taking part, and there was rarely a full station turn-out.

The *Book of the WAAF*, published in 1942, gives the reasons for this emphasis on Parades: 'A certain period of disciplinary training is necessary for efficiency

Going on Parade at Heslington, *c.* 1942. Note the Nissen huts and bicycle shelter (Dorothy Beasty)

and desirable for health and well-being. Drilling on the Parade ground in company with airmen gives the WAAF recruits an example and an incentive . . . Mentally, as well as physically, the recruits are stimulated.'

Many are the stories of disasters, large and small, which befell the marching airwomen. Returning from a route march at Bridgnorth, Barbara Hughes was very embarrassed when, 'I was in the centre lane and not really looking where I was going. Everyone else skirted the bollard at the gate, except me, and I went flying.'

'On dark mornings in the blackout, when we had to walk the length of Queen Street, Edinburgh, the back marker had to carry a lamp, and we felt like a long glowworm!'

At St Athan, Daphne Cole remembers a very frightening Drill Sergeant:

On a very windy day, as we marched, the wind blew our skirts up, which amused the passing airmen. As we tried to smooth our skirts down, the Sergeant shouted, 'I don't care if your bloody eyebrows drop off, keep your eyes front and leave your skirts alone!' At another time, due to the wind blowing his voice away from us, we failed to hear his 'About Turn'. After sheepishly marching back from the edge of the Parade ground, he greeted us with, 'Hello! Had a nice holiday?'

Mary Palmer at Cranwell remembers the considerable amusement derived from the music relayed over the Tannoy for the men and women on various courses marching back to their classes after their dinner break. 'The record was played by the Duty Officer, who set the time for the particular march chosen. Quite often he would neglect to adjust the timing, so that the music was often too fast or too slow, having a hilarious effect on the squads – sometimes it was sheer pandemonium. It was worse when the Officer tried to adjust it in mid-stream. Then the march ended in a shambles! Sometimes we Duty Clerks, did the same thing purposely to brighten up a dull day. It certainly livened things up!'

Those incidents were at training sessions. The real thing came at Commanding Officer's Weekly Parades or even more prestigious events. After one of the weekly marches past the flag at RAF Manby, Eve Hall was one of the airwomen standing to attention, waiting for the Commanding Officer's Inspection. 'Then the station band started playing and the Commanding Officer yelled out, "Will those b—— WAAF stop wriggling their feet in time to the music!"' At another Parade Inspection, a seagull relieved itself on Emily Ridley's friend. 'How I kept my face straight I'll never know, as the Group Captain came near us!' At a special Battle of Britain Parade at

Brandy Bay, Ann Welch 'was in the front rank of the March Past and got a wasp up my skirt! I think only my blackouts saved me – but I had to fall out rather hurriedly!'

Parades were also suitable occasions to announce, and give, special awards. After a very bad winter in 1944 at 16 MU Stafford, Mabel De Magalhaes Braz was in the Parade 'called to award a WAAF Corporal the Oakleaf and Mention in Despatches. When the Citation was read out, it stated that she had received the award, "For staying up all night with the plumber". Needless to say, everyone nearly had hysterics!'

While Mary Palmer and her friend were at work one day, the Warrant Officer came running in and detailed them to go and hoist the flag urgently as the Station Commander had arrived back unexpectedly.

We had never done any flag hoisting and as we rushed out the Warrant Officer shouted, 'Don't forget to salute'. However, as we were struggling with the ropes he called us back frantically, yelling, 'You haven't got your hats on'. Back we came and then back again to the hoisting. By this time we were laughing so much that we couldn't fathom which rope was which. Then we got the flag halfway up the mast where it stuck and fell back again.

March past after a Polish Investiture at Hemswell, 1944 (Kate Godfrey)

All this time the Warrant Officer was shouting instructions at us, but to no avail. Eventually he went out and did it himself.

Even less popular was the Church Parade, since it often broke up an airwoman's Rest Day. Girls also disliked being divided up into religious denominations, as Louie McGaughey explains:

At my first Church Parade in Gloucester, I remember someone shouting for the Roman Catholics to line up in one spot, Jews in another, Church of England in another and the ODs somewhere else. Being a Methodist, I did not know where I was supposed to go, so for that one day I joined the Church of England. Later when I was issued with my dog tags [identity discs], I saw that on them my religion was marked OD. I told the Corporal that I was nothing of the kind and she kindly explained that OD meant 'Other Denominations'. We Methodists, Baptists, Jehovah's Witnesses etc., were all lumped together as ODs.

An unusual feature struck Irene Park, when her 'OD Group proved to be almost entirely Church of Scotland, and we were, almost without exception, to pattern – medium height, plumpish and with reddish hair. Perhaps we, north of the tartan curtain, are more of a type than we realize!'

At her Church of England Parade, Joyce Barnes noted, 'after the usual forming up, standing in the biting wind and so on, we finally entered the church building, with frosty breath, red and dripping noses and hands too cold to open the hymn-book. To us, cold and miserable, was announced the first hymn, "Oh Happy Band of Pilgrims!"'

A young girl evangelist used to visit Olive Haughton's hut and the NAAFI. 'One night she asked us, "Have you found Jesus?" Quick as a flash, Wendy, a parson's daughter, said to her, "Why? Is he lost?" She was the camp comedian!'

The Padres of all denominations were a different matter, usually very approachable and well-liked by all personnel. Joyce Barnes reported back to her parents that her Padre called the girls 'roses among thorns', and Peggy Peak was much envied when she was prepared for Christening and then Confirmation by a Padre 'who was very handsome!'

When Vera Homer went to early Communion on Wednesday mornings, 'we had a great cooked breakfast laid on in the Sergeants' Mess. I never knew who called the most, the Lord or the Breakfast!'

Marching on Parade was often enlivened by a band, and most camps had at least one, which they cherished.

When Mary Young was stationed at the No. 10 Balloon Centre between 1939 and 1941, it was decided to try to form a WAAF Band.

A very glamorous RAF Officer and the Station Bugler taught us to play drums and bugle. We had no proper instruments but several propaganda marches outside the Officers' Mess convinced the Commanding Officer that we were serious. I had the big drum from the Dance Band slung round my neck on a piece of rope with a meat hook! The leopard [whose] skin I wore had been shot by one of the WAAF when she was living abroad. Eventually we had proper instruments, and sometimes we made so much noise that we missed the words of command and went straight on when everyone else had turned off!

The WAAF Band that never was – 'we were given instruments, badges etc., but never played, because the RAF Bandmaster objected'. Cranwell, 1943 (Phyllis Moore)

Gertrude Hodges remembered 'a Public Parade for Wings for Victory Week, in which the RAF Band at 16 MU was to take a prominent part. Then, only three days before it, the Drum Major went down with, of all things, measles! Panic! The bandsmen got together to petition the CO, saying that they would be willing to accept the WAAF Drum Major to lead them. "She's good!' [She led them and *was* good.]

Bandswomen were, however, of variable quality. On their Drum and Bugle March through Manchester, Margaret Scarlett overheard a watcher say, 'Those girls were chosen more for their looks than their music!' 'Well, we were not very talented,' she agrees.

'At Cranwell we had an RAF Band', says Mary Palmer, 'which was super, and also a WAAF Band which was bad. If you were marching in the front line as marker behind this band, you ducked when the mace was thrown up, for it was not always caught!'

Monica Hughes was part of the RAF Crosby Drum and Bugle Band,

and I became a bugler. We wore a small brass harp on each sleeve. On Sundays I used to go to Mass at the Roman Catholic church, have breakfast and then head the Church of England Parade. As we went up this rather steep hill, the bugles used to falter a bit, but we soon recovered.

One day I went to a Tea Dance at the Astoria ballroom [still in uniform, worn at all times]. When the band leader saw my harps, he became very interested. I think he thought I played the instrument and it would nicely fill a gap in his band! Alas! I couldn't help him out! He looked very wistful, but his band looked after me pretty well afterwards.

Another so-called Parade was when service personnel received their pay. The WAAF said it was only once a fortnight because it was so small, being only two-thirds of RAF airmen's pay. When Joan Pierce, a Plotter, first joined the WAAF in 1943, she received 14s a week.

I was housed, clothed and fed of course, but that 14 shillings had to stretch a long way.

We had to buy our own shoe polish, button polish, soap, toothpaste, notepaper, stamps, face powder, lipstick and cream, as well as pay for our cigarette and chocolate rations each week. Also, in spite of reasonable meals on camp, being young we were always hungry, and spent a lot on food in the

NAAFI and in the cafés of the nearest towns. We had to pay for cinema tickets (camp cinemas were usually 6*d*), our bus fares to the nearest town, if we weren't lucky enough to hitch a lift, and our fares home on a 48-hour pass. Then we liked to buy a pair of thinner lisle stockings 'for best' if we could, and extra collars. No wonder we were always broke, and letters home regularly included requests for money. Our Post Office Savings Books were withdrawn very often.

At her first Pay Parade, which was held in a disused hangar, Peggy Watson, in an attempt to impress her Sergeant with her smartness, found

the concrete floor in many places was very shiny and slippery, and as I came to a halt my foot slipped. Down I went, grabbing the blanket covering the table on which the money was piled. Coins went rolling in all directions and notes flew around like butterflies. The men including the Paying Officer were immediately down on their knees in an effort to retrieve the money. It all had to be recounted of course, which delayed things somewhat. As for myself. Well! After I had picked myself up, I simply froze. No one said anything to me, other than Sergeant Brylcream (our nickname because of his hair) but even he could not find adjectives applicable. One way or another, I had certainly impressed him!

A particular Pay Parade is mentioned by Joan Arnold. 'When our name was called we answered "Sir", followed by the last three figures of our service number. We had a very nervous ginger-headed airwoman, with a speech impediment that had to be heard to be believed! Her name was Lyall and the last three figures of her number 767. Poor thing! We always giggled when her name was called!'

Winifred Smith attended a Pay Parade where one of the girls fainted onto a fire hydrant, which went off covering everyone with foam. 'Eventually an airman was summoned to remove it as it was too heavy for the girls to even lift!'

Working in Pay Accounts at Manby during the demobilization period, Una Cooke was given the Polish contingent to pay.

Prior to taking them, I was faced, to my dismay, with all the unpronounceable names which I had to call out. So I contacted the RAF Corporal, who had previously taken it, to find out how to pronounce the names – and I put each name in phonetics in pencil in the margin.

The first time for this parade was quite awesome, held in a huge hangar, rather dark, with all the men lined up, and the pay table with two RAF

Officers and myself at one end under a single spotlight. It was unnerving to say the least! Then I started on the list, and, hey presto, everyone answered to his name – to my surprise!

> Yet there are precious hours of leave
> And leisure moments granted,
> Each like a small oasis seems,
> And every hour enchanted!

Like Pat Sparks who sent this poem, and Margaret Eversley who wrote it, this must have been the feeling of most airwomen when they reached a period of leave. In theory they were entitled to a week after three months' work, but in practice it didn't always work out, sometimes because of their own devotion to their Section needs or because the events of war intervened. Whatever happened, it was enjoyably anticipated, as were the two free Travel Warrants a year.

'On my first leave', says Wendy Twyman,

I was far too shy and frightened of the journey. On the Underground, I happened to mention that I was worried in finding my way to my railway station, to another girl. A man sitting nearby overheard and said, 'Don't worry,

Off duty antics in the snow, Heaton Park, 1943.
(The Lancaster pilot crashed and died in Holland in 1944) (Margaret Gleeson)

luv. I'll see you get there safely!' Just a stranger, but somehow we trusted people then! He took me round to the station in time for the last train home.

In the carriage a very tired soldier was sitting. I told him to go to sleep and I would wake him before I got off. Everything was blacked out – stations, everything! Finally the train stopped. I woke the soldier and said 'Good luck! I'm going now,' and out I went – right down the embankment! For some reason the train hadn't pulled into the station. Luckily the Guard had seen me fall and helped me back. However, I had lost my hat and glasses, which I retrieved with my father next morning.

Another heart-warming story of a journey comes from Ann Welch:

With my kit bag, gas mask, tin hat and much trepidation, I joined eleven other Radar Operators at King's Cross on a bitterly cold day in February 1943. After Edinburgh and Inverness changes, we set off on a troop train to Wick. We were the only twelve girls aboard.

North of the Cairngorms the train stuck firmly in a snow drift. Then a bagpipe started to play and before we knew it, the train was full of Highland dancers. It was a marvellous way to keep warm and make friends. What a wonderful spirit there was! All young people fighting for our country – sailors going to Scapa Flow or Aberdeen to sail on Russian convoys; soldiers – the Black Watch, the Highland Light Infantry, Lovat Scots, Cameron Highlanders – all joining their various units to train for commando raids, service abroad or merely to guard our various Radar Stations; airmen going to Wick or the Orkneys, to Coastal Command, Photographic Reconnaissance, Fighter Stations and Meteorological Flights – all with a great sense of time going by and making the most of the precious days or weeks left to them. We were soon dancing our hearts out, up and down the train, and what fun it was!

After four hours the train began to move again. At a small station, the ladies from the WVS – bless them – produced hot tea for us. Just for the fun of it we all swapped hats; I wore a glengarry and a soldier wore my WAAF hat for the rest of the journey.

Theresa Richardson remembers a different kind of journey in a cattle train, travelling from Little Rissington to Stratford-upon-Avon to see a play on a free ticket. 'We ran to and fro and made animal noises, startling all the civvies en route,

Six photographers getting tea from a mobile YMCA van at Poulton, July 1944 (Nancy Griffin)

who must have thought we were lunatics!' But for every journey, there was always the chance of mishaps sometimes before it even began! An arrangement made by Hilda Brewer and her friend Anne, 'to meet under the clock at Waterloo Station and travel together to Cardington', went wrong:

> I waited but she never arrived. When I had crossed London to catch my train, it was just going out of sight. At the Traffic Office to get my pass signed [to prove she had been there], they sent me to spend the night at a hostel just outside the station. Here I was asked to share a bunk-bed with another late arrival. When I got to the room, there was Anne! We had both been waiting under the clock – me at Waterloo and she at Waterloo Junction!

It was also at Waterloo station, waiting for her train to Upavon, that Eileen Cunningham's travel bag 'suddenly shot open and the contents were strewn on the ground. I found myself surrounded by men of the three services coming to my aid to help retrieve my belongings, including my service undies. Was my face red!'

On her way back from a weekend pass there was an air raid over London, and by the time Ann Sinclair reached Chippenham,

it was gone midnight and the next train not until 7 a.m. The station was crowded with airmen, and the stationmaster came to us and said that as there was only one small waiting room, he thought we ought to have it for the rest of the night. So, escorting me and my friend inside, he carefully locked the door, much to our delight. It was a kindly gesture and much more comfortable than spending the night outside on the open platform. We must have looked very young and tired.

About to be met outside Glasgow station by friends from her Balloon site, Jean Nabb had a frightening experience:

It was a slightly foggy night, and as I began to cross the road to my colleagues they called to me that they were going to a snack bar to get us a treat. I was to wait outside. Then I saw the forms approaching. They were youths and they were encircling me on three sides . . . and closing in on me. Then another youth pushed his way through, saying in a broad Glaswegian accent, 'What have I said about these lassies? Leave her alone. She's a serving lassie!'

Just then my friends arrived, with toffee apples of all things! Realizing something was amiss, they came running towards me. The leader of the gang then asked us how far we had to go to catch our tramcar and detailed some of his boys to escort us. All I could think was that it was fortunate that this particular gang had some respect for the job we were doing.

Though there was always a residue of hostility to women in uniform, great friendliness and support were also displayed to service people by a large part of the population, including royalty. Once a week Queen Mary used to come to Margaret Wilson's camp cinema at Hullavington to see the film.

A red cloth was put on the front seat for her. When Christmas came, a few of us were invited to her cottage. On arriving, the butler let us in and after singing carols, we were offered wine and Christmas cake. She was a real, stately Queen and very gracious. She often gave a lift to people on the camp, who were walking the six miles back. I was thrilled one evening when I was invited into the limousine with my friend. She talked to us and we both received a medal to prove we had been in the car.

Many others posted in this area were given lifts by the Queen, who was always concerned about their welfare!

In another incident Vicki Raine discloses that 'If we didn't wish to stay at YWCA hostels on taking 48-hour leaves from London, we could apply to the Soldiers', Sailors' and Airmen's Families Association (SSAFA) in order to take advantage of hospitality in private homes.' In this way Marjorie Bradford encountered the kindness of two Welsh sisters, 'who invited us to their home and gave us delicious rabbit pie, a cosy chair by a real fire and tea from bone-china cups and saucers – such a joy after the NAAFI.'

One night, unable to take her two airwomen on a Sleeping Out Pass from Middle Wallop, a friend arranged for Joyce Mollett and companion

to spend the night with a Major and his wife at the big house. We had packed our night clothes and sponge bag in a carrier-bag each. The butler answered the door and solemnly handed them over the parlour maid. Later we found our bags unpacked and our hot-water bottles in the bed. They fed us and treated us as if we were their own family.

How to hitch a lift. Spitalgate, 1943 (Phyllis Moore)

A seaplane tender was another form of transport.
Mountbatten, 1945 (Kate Godfrey)

Service personnel always did a lot of free hitching from place to place. One day, however, Joyce Mollett thought her end had come

when, having a lift in the back of a lorry, driven by a young Pilot Officer, he told me to jump out. It was far too high for me in my tight service skirt to even get my leg over the ledge. He spurred me on and said he would catch me when I jumped. So I jumped and we clung together for what seemed to be forever, waltzing backwards down the road, until we felt safe on our feet. He got back into the lorry limply, and my friend of the time, still convulsed with laughter, saluted him as he drove off.

For airwomen stranded at awkward hours, without bus or train to their station, as often happened, it was necessary to find other modes of travel. Arriving in thick fog at Holmes Chapel, Betty McMullen had no transport to take her to her camp. 'A gentleman saw my plight and said, "If you don't mind travelling in the hearse, I can drop you right at the gates of Cranage". We slowly made our way through the country lanes. It was rather weird to say the least. Arriving, we drove right through the gates to the Guardroom, causing quite a stir!'

At Kidbrooke, Mary Hodges' room-mate 'asked me to go to the shops with her. About two doors away was a chauffeur-driven Rolls Royce. The driver asked us if we would like a lift. When we hesitated, he said, "It's all right! I've been told to pick up anyone in uniform." We got in. It was very grand and I'm afraid we went further than we intended, so we had a long walk back. But it was worth it!' Sheila Parker also remembers a lift on the same journey in a dustcart, followed by one in a Rolls Royce; 'uniform being the open sesame to such kindness'.

It was also a code among service people to help one another. Once, outside Colchester, Muriel Hodson had a lift in a lorry

driven by the blackest negro I had ever seen [probably a member of the United States Army Air Force stationed in Britain]. 'Hop in', he said. 'There are plenty of your pals in the back of the trailer.' There were! Pilots, army women of the Auxiliary Territorial Service (ATS), soldiers, and NAAFI civilian personnel. He drove like mad and we had to hang on to the boxes we were sitting on. When we got out we thanked the driver. 'Those Kipper Boxes don't smell much,' we commented. 'Kipper Boxes!,' said he. 'There is only one. The rest is ammunition!'

5
AT LEISURE

Despite the gloomy news bulletins and the busy workday of their duties, airwomen threw themselves into all kinds of activities with infectious enthusiasm during their free time on camp.

Theatre was the lifeblood of most stations, large and small, and gave opportunities for men and women to mix informally, without the usual barriers of rank.

In Coastal Command at Northwood, Gwendoline Whipps was one of a concert party which involved airmen and airwomen. 'We did sketches, songs, dances and mad pantomimes. Costumes were provided by an Officer with theatrical connections. Our backcloths were painted by a civilian in the Mapping Office. These shows were vastly more popular than productions by visiting entertainers from ENSA [the Entertainments National Service Association].'

'We put on shows each year for the camp,' declares Joyce Mollett.

Of course it meant giving up free time, but it was worth it to hear a large hall full of men, laughing at our antics!

One year we did a circus. I had to be browned all over as I was the fairy on the back of a 'horse'. I had a star on my head and a white ballet dress, which unfortunately had no tights. I borrowed a large pair of panties, but it worried me dreadfully that at the end, I had to kneel on one leg only, right in front of the stage.

During the Adjutant's long-winded speech at the end, the front part of the horse began to faint. Just in time the curtain went down. Then we found we couldn't remove the head. After a struggle we finally got the airman out, revived him, and then put him together again for our photograph.

While Edith Frank was on the Isle of Man, each particular watch ran a dance once a month followed by an entertainment.

At one it was announced that ACW Gwen Neale would sing 'One Fine Day' from the opera *Madam Butterfly*, at which the Commanding Officer's

Taking a bow. A Station Variety Show at Duxford, 1940 (Jill Nielson)

face bore a rather pained expression. What he did not know was that ACW
Neale (née Veevers) had been with CEMA [the Council for Encouragement
of Music and the Arts] prior to enlisting, that she was a Gold Medal winner
from the Royal Manchester College of Music and had a wonderful voice.
His expression at the end of her aria was very different, and the applause
from the hall was deafening.

A famous person known for his Gang Shows was Squadron Leader Ralph
Reader, who went to Acklington while Monica Hughes was there. 'He produced
a show where I found I could give a good high kick as a chorus girl, and I was
also in quite a few sketches. The show went down very well, and needless to say,
especially the chorus line.'

Straight drama, too, had its place, as in the play *Mirror to Elizabeth* – such
patriotic subjects were always popular, as well as the historical settings which
allowed the cast to dress up. In this particular play Marie Kenyon took the part of
one of the six ladies in waiting.

During a tense scene, the Queen stood centre stage in all her Elizabethan
finery, holding a large sword and in a towering rage. Now, our stage at

Ouston was very small, so, when Elizabeth, shouting, 'God, that I were a man to go out and fight, fight . . .' punctuated her speech with wild sweeps of her sword, we ladies in waiting had to take a smart one, two, back, to avoid being decapitated. A great roar of laughter rose from the audience and we lost the atmosphere completely.

At Cranwell, states Mary Palmer, 'We also had our own rep company, with Leslie Sands and Peter Sallis. They gave us first-class productions.' For those lucky enough to be able to reach London, like Vicki Raine, 'we were always able to get free theatre tickets and we saw many West End plays that way, as well as making good use of all the Service Clubs there'.

At some ENSA concerts which Kathlyn Bell attended, 'mostly very good, there were sometimes comedians with incredibly filthy humour. Our male Flight Sergeant told me not to laugh so uproariously at their jokes, – he said it was unladylike. He did not realize that I was only laughing because everyone else was – I didn't understand any of it!' On another occasion, Joan Arnold was present when 'Gracie Fields sang "Ave Maria" and "Bless This House" to a completely silent audience in our huge hangar.'

According to Mary Palmer, Cranwell was a good camp for entertainment. However,

many ENSA shows were made hilarious, not by the performers, but by the remarks fired at them by the audience. One show included an act called 'The Peaches on Parade' – about a dozen oversize women, singing and dancing in satin dresses. The audience encored them in a rather cruel send-up way. I also recall a really super production of *Heartbreak House* with Robert Donat.

One day a ripple went round that a French ENSA party was coming, and of course all the men had visions of the can-can, etc. It was almost impossible to get tickets. On the night, shock of shocks, it turned out to be a *cultural* French show, and we all sat through classical music and French solos. That was the quietest ENSA I ever went to!

The Council for the Encouragement of Music and the Arts (CEMA) and other bodies, like the YWCA, organized musical evenings for those interested and Monica Hughes became a member of a camp club that met to play their own classical records. The occasional 'Music while You Work' catered for less highbrow tastes.

A concert party at West Malling, featuring the Harmony Group (Gwendoline Voase)

There were, of course, other things for girls to do to entertain themselves. At Marham, Daphne Light took part in weekly whist drives. At Invergordon, three airwomen and Una Cooke won a quiz between the RAF and the WAAF – 'a big occasion on stage in the NAAFI in which the prize was 2s 6d in savings stamps each. We thought that quite a prize too!' At Dora Hatch's camp,

occasionally debates were held and these could be very interesting. Being also a member of the camp church choir, I attended choir practice once a week and cleaned the church brass. At Christmas, five of us went carol singing in the village. We received abuse from one man, who said that we should be at the front, but everyone else seemed to enjoy our carols, and at one house we were invited in and the man played the piano as we sang. Unfortunately there were no mince pies or wine to replenish us, but we were given a contribution to our collection for the local hospital.

At Catterick, a friend of Dilys Upton's father 'gave an evening talk on ornithology.

He said he was delighted to see so many people interested in birds. He had no idea that we had all been detailed to attend.'

949 Balloon Squadron at Crewe had quite an active hobby interest. The Group Headquarters at one time held an exhibition in Manchester, where everybody, including Mary Undrum, 'was encouraged to make something – knitted, sewn, painted, woodworked etc. I knitted a tiny rabbit without a pattern, and won the First Prize for knitted toys, amongst the huge knitted elephants, dogs, cats, tigers, etc.'

In the civilian world Monica Hughes discovered that 'the doors of church and YWCA halls were always open to us, and in those places we could get a cup of tea, snacks and usually a good game of table tennis or snooker.'

Another popular form of entertainment was dancing. People often described the girls of this era as 'dance mad' – but it was a perfect relaxation for mixed company. In Daphne Light's estimation, 'All-ranks dances were wonderful – admission 6d, spirits 1s, beer about 4d. The band included musicians from famous dance bands and we had Steve Race as pianist at RAF Marham in 1943.' 'Dances

Handicraft class, Pitreavie, 1943 (Mary Ker)

Three services dancing at the Nuffield Centre, London, 1940. There were seldom enough men at that time
(Mary Pearce)

at the NAAFI, where the beer seemed to flow like water', are recalled by Kathlyn
Bell, together with 'marvellous station bands of really professional standard'. In
the memory of Joan Arnold, 'there were "the Squadronaires" and "the Blue
Boys" bands to jive to. Happy, happy days and nights.'

The big deal at Joy Moulds' station of Biggin Hill 'was to hitch a ride to
London and go dancing at Covent Garden – then a beautiful ballroom. A big floor
was laid over the orchestra stalls and the stage, in a figure of eight. Ivy Benson's All
Girl Band played afternoons and evenings. I am still meeting Canadians and
Americans who remember the Garden. What days!'

As the war progressed and the majority of Englishmen were in the services
abroad, Doreen May's dates 'were increasingly with Australian, Canadian, Polish
and American Air Force types, but war ended abruptly many romances . . .'.
When the Americans arrived, Joyce Barrett was among 'the large numbers of
WAAF invited to dances on their camps, where they put lorries on to convey us
back and forth. At Christmas, I remember seeing a decorated Christmas tree
15 feet high, which had been flown over especially from the States.' Such

generosity was not always welcome, as Eva Cormacey notes: 'The American GIs were very liberal with their chocolates, sweets, and biscuits, which tended to cause a little jealousy among our own airmen.' Initiation into jitterbugging for Marjorie Blake was 'at the camp dance at Duxford, when a very tall gangling coloured American asked me to dance. The next minute I was up in the air, then through his legs, lost my grip on his hands and went skidding across the dance floor in a most unwaffy-like manner. He didn't ask me again!'

Cinema shows were always popular. At Mary Palmer's station, 'we had our own cinema. Films changed twice a week and we had all the latest ones.' At most it only cost service personnel 6d, and they would travel long distances to their nearest town if there were no cinemas on camp.

Nevertheless, on small remote stations or Radar sites, as Stella Cottman explains, 'there were no medical or NAAFI facilities nor entertainment. But sometimes there was unintentional amusement when we were supplied with an infrequent film show – *The China Seas* with Clark Gable, was one such – when the film broke down regularly, with resulting cheering and catcalls.'

Though most avoided it if they could do so, the select few who were good at it enjoyed the many opportunities the RAF gave for sport. Games afternoons became very pleasant for Vicki Raine: 'I discovered early that if numbers were not right, the ones not chosen could sit on the grass and watch rather than partake. I liked that.' Others found that by hiding in a swimming cubicle, 'you could miss PT'.

Tennis, however, was an exception since most girls could play. On Dora Hatch's station, 'there were several hard tennis courts and I enjoyed playing. We also had badminton courts, a table-tennis table on the camp YWCA and a hockey-team.'

Games were usually segregated. Nevertheless, one day Joyce Meeks was asked

by the male hockey team of my squadron to make up their team with another airwoman, in a match against another male hockey team. I had never played hockey with men before. Their idea was to smash the ball as hard as possible, without worrying about hockey stick above the shoulder, and then charge hell for leather after it. Unfortunately, being a half-back, I was hit by the ball, once on the shin and once on the thigh. By the time I went home that weekend, I had two tennis-ball-size bruises all colours of the rainbow. My mum was shocked. Ordered me not to play with those rough airmen again!

It was ironic! Here was I, a 19–20 year old, away from home for the first time, doing a highly secret job of helping to spy on the enemy [she was a

WAAF Inter-Services Tennis Team, Northern Ireland, 1944. The Captain, Queenie Allen, was a Badminton International while LACW Huey, on the back row, right, was an Irish Hockey International (Lesley Nightingale)

Signals Clerk at Chicksands Priory processing Enigma codes] and there I was being told off by my mum. Moreover, because of the stress on secrecy, none of my family ever knew what my job was.

Daphne Donelly, another airwomen at least willing to give it a try, 'was invited to play hockey, and they put me in goal. I was petrified, and when the ball trickled towards me, I gave a wild swipe and missed! They didn't ask me again.'
At the Command Shooting Championships at Bisley, two WAAF, one of whom was Barbara Peters, were competing with their team.

There was a fair in the local village. So the men from our station took us down to visit it and steered us towards the shooting gallery. After shooting everything in sight, the demented stallholder pleaded with us to go away, as we were putting his potential customers off! Our Station Commander, also in our team, was so amused that he stood in a fish and chip queue to reward us with much needed sustenance.

A humorous look at a netball game comes from Phyllis Smart:

Our netball team is awfully good,
We play the village girls,
We throw the ball and jump around
With graceful twists and twirls.

I play games very well myself,
My passing ball is neat,
And when I leap, I always land
On someone else's feet!

Time off produced many other diversions. An airman was trying to teach Joan Slater 'to drive on one of the RAF trucks. I had been given one or two lessons and thought I wasn't doing too badly, until one day, when I was driving down the runway, I happened to look up, and saw a plane coming in to land on the runway that crossed ours. I froze and shut my eyes. My instructor swore and grabbed the wheel, and that was the end of that! I still can't drive.'

On another occasion when short of money – a regular occurrence – Cherry Symonds and a friend 'decided to raise some extra cash by collecting empty mineral bottles left behind the seats at the camp picture house. We stuffed them inside the top of our battledress. On the way back to our billet, and bulging at the seams, we came face to face with a WAAF Officer. With great difficulty, we tore off a salute, accompanied by a loud chinking of glass.'

When she was off camp, Elizabeth Andrews was annoyed to discover that 'walking down a certain street in Eastbourne, irrespective of day or night, I was always wolf-whistled. Eventually my boyfriend traced the source. It was a parrot!'

A sadder tale came from Joyce Curtis:

One free Sunday, while I was at Euston House, my friend and I were asked by a Corporal to go to St Dunstan's to take a patient for a walk. We went, and it was tragic to see all the young men, either limbless or blind, sitting around trying to take tea. We were asked to have some, but we couldn't face the fact that we were so able, as against these poor struggling men.

Then we took this young man – Bob – for a walk in Regent's Park. He had been blinded in a landing in Norway. He could smell the flowers blooming in the garden, but what hurt me so, was that I was ignorant of the names of those he asked me to describe.

The girls sought to enliven their days with parties of many kinds. Since a Radar watch of about thirty girls all worked and lived together, Mavis Pickford found that 'short off-duty recreation tended to end up with large groups going out together dancing, going to the pictures, shopping or having tea in a local "Olde English Tea Shoppe" – such a change from the tin mugs in the Mess. In Uxbridge at Christmas there would be some sort of party or dance. In the early days young male members of the watch would join the groups and many romances resulted, including my own.'

A similar situation is described by Pat Sparks:

We were a friendly group of girls, about forty of us in a large house. When I hear of girls not being able to live in harmony, I think back to those happy, friendly days. I can't remember a time when there was any trouble or bickering, and in fact it was usually the other way – we shared our troubles and heartaches and did our best to help. We set each other's hair, gave manicures, plucked eyebrows and generally helped each other. We often gave parties and then we would all chip in to help prepare – the times I have made jellies with golden syrup and gelatine!

In the words of Joan Arnold, 'Our social life was great! Forty-seven parties in thirty nights!'

Sometimes high spirits were a little too high! At one party, to which the MT Section invited the Signals Section, among whose number was Sybil Stansfield, 'one MT driver became over-zealous and merry and tried to dive off a table into the fire bucket. She broke her ankle, and the best we could do was remove the hut door from its hinges and slow march her upon it the 400 yards to the Sick Bay – not looked upon very kindly by the Medical Officer!'

In another incident Joyce Williams recalls, 'attending a party at the Sergeants' Mess, at which the Officers had been invited. In the early hours of the morning, the most unpopular Officer, a Squadron Leader, rather the worse for drink, was unceremoniously placed by the RAF Sergeants in the cab of a heavy goods vehicle on its way to Shap Fell, the driver having been stopped and informed that the Officer needed a lift to Kendal . . .!'

'Three of our girls had a 21st Birthday,' wrote Laura Lee,

and they were very upset to find that all leave had been cancelled at that time [it was about a year before D-Day]. So we all planned to give them a party. I got permission from the Commanding Officer for us to be allowed to wear civilian dress for the occasion and we all sent home for all the food they could spare. [One Scottish girl's mother sent a whole salmon in a rush basket!] We decorated the NAAFI and all sat down to a lovely spread, followed by games and a sing-song. All the Officers were there and the climax came when our Flight Officer presented a silver cross and chain to the three who were 21!

Invergordon had wonderful countryside to explore and Una Cooke loved cycling around with her friends and swimming in the sea.

The WAAF Birthday 1943 was an especially enjoyable day. We had a Treasure Hunt covering miles around. A very clever LACW in our midst (actually an Oxford graduate, who later became a Meteorological Officer) had organized the clues in rhyme – to be found in odd places. The local people must have wondered why all the RAF and WAAF were 'flying' hither and thither on cycles! My friend and I won it – I can't remember the prize. After the Treasure Hunt we had a big birthday cake and a lovely spread (for those days!) buffet-style in the NAAFI, followed by a dance. The room looked like a glasshouse at Kew, as we had decorated it all over with greenery from the woods.

At another camp, Eileen Tregellis remembers:

as there were eight of us airwomen, we palled up together and called ourselves Our Gang. We used to hire cycles in the village of Llantwit Major for 6d or 1s half day, and we had a lovely time exploring down all the country lanes. Of course we were in battledress, but a notice went up on camp saying that no battledress must be worn off camp. This meant wearing a jacket and skirt – not very good for cycling. Some of the girls sent home for shorts. In the summer we would sneak out through a gap in the hedge, pick up the shorts from the man who hired us the bikes and change behind the hedges.

We had a great time. In a place they called the Bungalow they served teas. Everyone had to wait for a seat to get sausages, home-grown tomatoes, fried bread and chips for about 1s 3d. Also our shorts got us wolf-whistled. At other times, as eggs were scarce, if any of us were going on leave we took ourselves off on the bike and went round the farms getting an odd egg here and there. They used to charge 1d each. We did enjoy ourselves, all pals together.

Airwoman in battledress (Valerie Kitchener)

Some airwomen, like Pauline King, were very fortunate to have a particularly considerate Officer in charge:

Because we worked long hours in the Equipment Section, our Officer would book a room at the local pub now and again, where he would order sandwiches. Then we would all spend a happy relaxed evening and wobble back to camp on our service cycles by 2300 hours, quite refreshed and ready for another day.

At Wittering, where Mary Mackay was stationed in 1942,

many of us became friendly with Bomber Command crews at nearby airfields. The central point for all meetings was Stanford, particularly at the Millstone – a very cosy old pub. I can still recall the tension when it was all too quiet and deserted and we knew they were out on a raid. Nobody said anything – even the publican and local people knew, and there was an understanding between everybody.

The next night we used to creep in with fixed smiles, wondering whose face would be missing and dreading to ask about a particular person. It became commonplace to make only casual arrangements, we never dared to make definite dates. Often I heard the girls in the same billet crying in the night (I think I did myself) but generally they would just say that so and so had 'bought it' last night (knowing he was dead).

Since much of their work revolved so closely around planes and their occupants, many airwomen – being very given to writing poetry – often sought to express their feelings in verse – or near-poetry. Here Una Cooke describes some of her station planes:

The aircraft at Alness were Sunderlands and Catalina Flying Boats. It was a lovely sight in the early morning – the line of those Flying Boats, right down the centre of the Firth, glistening in the early sunshine. Then, when they took off one after another, they were like huge white birds, skimming along and gradually lifting off the water.

To most of the airwomen, like Greta Briggs, the pilots were their heroes:

> He is so young and joyous, yet he bears,
> The fate of Nations on his shoulders now.
> His roaring Spitfire thunders up the sky –
> To him the drone of engines seems a song.
> He rides the cloud pavilioned lists, that lie
> Between earth's surface and the evening star.
> His feats of arms are such as men have dared
> Never before. His brief reports can vie
> With all the ballads of those knights and kings,
> Whose deeds were red-hot news in Camelot.
> He has a threefold England in his charge:
> The old-world England we have loved so long,
> And then the splendid England of today,
> And finally the England yet to be.
> We pass him in the street – a knight who wears
> Not golden spurs, perhaps – but shining wings!

Inevitably, with their new freedom and in the heightened atmosphere of living for the moment, romance blossomed for the youthful WAAF. However, there were often difficulties of one kind or another.

On 14 February 1943 Ann Welch received two telegrams:

Portraits of pilots in 611 West Lancashire Squadron by WAAF artist Elva Blacker (Alice Findlay)

The first one was from Richard to say he was arriving at Wick in the one and only train next day, having two days' leave. The other was from Derek saying exactly the same thing, and both asked me to get the day off on compassionate grounds. Rather difficult! I suspected that they were both going to ask me to marry them, and I really didn't know which to accept! Looking back now, I could have told myself that it shouldn't have been either. If I'd really loved one of them, I'd have known, wouldn't I?

There was a similar embarrassment for Gweneth Malby when, 'in October at West Raynham, I was called to the Administration Office one day, to receive a telegram. It read: "Will you marry me?" and had a pre-paid reply for one word! Of course the admin staff knew what the message was. Later that month Jack had a few days Embarkation Leave, so I was granted "passionate", i.e. Compassionate Leave, and we became engaged, with the wedding two months later.'

In any emergency it was always heartening to see the way that airwomen bent over backwards to help one another. 'One of our friends was to follow her French-Canadian fiancé out to Canada,' explains Winifred Smith, a Parachute Packer:

A wedding dress designed by Winifred Smith (Winifred Smith)

She couldn't borrow an Air Ministry wedding dress, as she was marrying over there. So we collected the best silk panels from a 'chute returned from France. Then we set to work. A final fitting came, when the WAAF Duty Officer walked into our Repair Section. There standing on the table was this lovely vision in ivory, creamy-white silk. The Officer had been wondering why we had been working so late, and we breathed a sigh of relief when she complimented us on the wedding gown. I made a second for another friend when her Chindit fiancé arrived suddenly. I was able to attend *her* wedding and see her safely married to her handsome Chindit.

Commenting on the reaction of men when airwomen began to use their Messes, Ann Osborne felt they were all in favour. 'I had many dates, in fact I married one! Everything was set for my wedding on 9 June 1944. The marriage was to take place at 3 o'clock in the afternoon at Northcoates church. We all arrived at the appointed hour but we waited for the vicar in vain. Eventually the best man went to the vicarage. And there he found the vicar digging his vegetable patch. He had forgotten about the marriage! But everything turned out well in the end.'

For Irene Smith, 'life at Heaton Park was very varied. Once, I was asked to give away one of the Corporals at her wedding. It was a quiet affair, just friends from the camp. I wonder if anyone has heard of a woman being best man before?'

6
WE SAW IT HAPPEN

[The extracts that follow are only a small selection from the many letters I have received from wartime airwomen – showing the highly responsible and important work they did while serving in the RAF.]

These are the words of airwomen at their work, who unwittingly encountered dramatic history in the making:

Dunkirk: 1940

GERTRUDE HODGES MT DRIVER RAF SWINGATE, DOVER

From our cliff-edge post we could look right down into Dover harbour. Through April and May refugee fishing fleets were dropping anchor within its shelter. Each morning it was obvious that yet more of them had arrived during the night, until the harbour was absolutely crammed . . .

Towards the end of May, Hawkinge issued a rifle and sixty rounds of ammunition to the Commer (my van), on condition it was taken off every time the WAAF driver (me) took over, since all members of the WAAF are guaranteed non-combatant by Act of Parliament, and they could not risk one of them being found armed by the invading forces when they came!

By the end of May we were getting air-raid sirens and all-clears on an average about five times a day. We lived the whole time with our tin hats beside us in readiness! . . .

Calais was in flames for five whole days before Churchill told the world . . . On the fifth day Churchill's now famous speech reached us from our radio.

Then one morning, arriving at the cliff-edge post, we found the harbour empty. ALL THE SHIPS WERE GONE! This must have been 27 May. Hawkinge Orderly Room told us that they had not all been refugee ships, as we had imagined . . . and that they had gone off in the night to attempt the rescue of our armies from the dunes between Calais and Dunkirk . . .

After handover at 5 p.m., I drove to the crossroads at the top of St Margaret's Bay. Looking down from our 300 ft cliff-top vantage, the Channel was full of small ships moving in all directions, supposedly picking their way through the minefields, while fast small units of the Royal Navy were darting here and there, like sheepdogs herding their flock.

VERA MORTIMER   MT DRIVER   UPAVON

The day started as usual in the MT (Transport) Yard but about 11 a.m., the Sergeant ordered one of the airmen to drive a lorry to several local farms and requisition several bales of hay. We were curious, and I asked the Sergeant if we were about to change to horses from aircraft? The hay arrived and was taken to empty huts and scattered over the floor. Later in the afternoon army lorries arrived at the yard, conveying soldiers who had landed that morning from the Dunkirk beaches. The hay, we discovered, was to be used instead of mattresses!

SYLVIA SWINBURNE   ADMINISTRATION   ST EVAL

The silence in the Sergeants' Mess, I well remember, as the news was received of the fall of France, for we realized invasion could be imminent. A Password had to be known each day. We were much amused when the WAAF Duty Officer and her NCO had forgotten the day's Password and were marched to the Guard House at the end of a bayonet!

The Enemy Have Landed: July 1940

GERTRUDE HODGES   MT DRIVER   RAF SWINGATE, DOVER

On the night of 11 July, I was sent to fetch the Civilian Engineer to the Operations Room, and thence back alone to the Guard Room to sign myself in, where the Wardens had a cup of tea waiting for me. Captain Dempsey sauntered in and advised me to stand by, because I might be needed. So I subsided onto the wicker waste-paper basket, tucked away between the door and the phone table. Thus we had our own Flight Lieutenant Commanding Officer (RAF), Captain Dempsey (Army) and Captain T— (Local Defence Volunteers) occupying the three chairs, while an Army Lieutenant, our RAF Warrant Officer, two uniformed Air Ministry Wardens and one plainclothes man were standing behind them, with the light from one low slung desk lamp casting an eerie colour from its green glass shade. . . . The phones were going repeatedly

An eyewitness sketch of the scene in Swingate Guardroom on the night of
11/12 July 1940 (Gertrude Hodges)

from ack-ack posts; from infantry posts; and from our radio posts. . . . It didn't
take me long to realize that these phone calls were reporting the dropping of
German parachutes and the subsequent destruction of them or actual capture
of their men and arms containers as they grounded. . . . It was all very
business-like – one batch after another of these parachutes and their personnel
being written off. They were not being dropped in large enough numbers to
constitute an army, just in tens and twenties.

Amid all this, Captain Dempsey's words came slowly as he marked the spot
on the map before him. 'Eight parachutes dropped at . . . One much larger
than the rest, carrying a dark object too big to be a man or arms container –
probably a small tank. No arms container with this lot? Right.' He picked up
another phone and repeated it. In the small room and unreal atmosphere,
there were remarks, orders and phones with still more parachutes.

Soon after two o'clock something came over the phone which had an
electric effect on the Guard Room. 'NOW'! Everything was instant activity.
The sudden clatter of rifles and tin hats; everyone tightening belts and
adjusting ammunition webbing. . . . As I crossed to the Commer, Captain

Dempsey said, 'We shan't want your vehicle, driver . . . We're going on foot. They're on the Downs behind us this time!'

On the next day the cliff-edge post was off the air and off the phone. Two days later, my afternoon's run took the Station Medical Orderly to the military hospital over at Sandgate. He came out an hour later looking rather shocked and thoughtful. . . . He remarked that they had a whole lot more wounded Germans in there. 'Shot up no end they were! Funny isn't it to be bringing wounded prisoners so far east again?'

Then Murphy in our barrack hut, recounting the glories of her current boyfriend. 'So funny! Bert says four Jerry soldiers they got in the Guard Room up there! . . . Bert says they had seventeen at first, but the others have already been sent off to a prisoners' camp' . . .

It was all hushed up in each case but I realized that cumulatively they all added up to the one incident!

SYLVIA SWINBURNE   WAAF G   ST EVAL

After the fall of France, there was always the fear of invasion from the air, and camps were protected by the RAF regiment. The Colonel in charge of St Eval decided that WAAF Officers should be given instruction in the use of arms. We therefore were taught how to use rifle, tommy gun, pistol and hand grenade. One Code and Cypher Officer was quite hopeless at

WAAF on weapon training for expected invasion, St Eval, 1940 (Sylvia Swinburne)

throwing, and when we were in a sandbagged pit learning to throw hand grenades, she always managed to drop the dummy grenades at our feet. Our horror can be imagined when we started to throw live grenades after removing the pin! Yet I live to tell the tale, much to my surprise!

Battle of Britain: 1940

SADIE YOUNGER FILTERER BENTLEY PRIORY

I can remember working flat out on the Estuary/Channel area of the Filter Room table. The heavy enemy attacks, meant for London, were continuous, apart from a lull at midday. Radar stations passed mass plots to Plotters, working at high speed, and Tellers were doubled up, as there was so much information to be passed to Operations Rooms. I needed both hands to filter tracks. I even remember telling the Controller on the dais that the heights on enemy raids could be anything between 15,000 and 25,000, but the weather was fine and the visibility good. All the squadrons from 11 and 12 Groups were airborne and on 15 September the Luftwaffe suffered its heaviest losses in many weeks. This was some kind of peak, a turning of the tide!

VERA SHAW PLOTTER 11 GROUP HEADQUARTERS, UXBRIDGE

15 September 1940. Early duty. Lovely day dawning, though trouble expected. Around 8 a.m. warning from Command of a big raid. It came! 250 plus aircraft approaching Dover. Plots came thick and fast. Soon table covered with raids. Noise indescribable – why must everyone shout so? Squadron board shows all squadrons in combat. Final score 185 shot down, and 26 of ours. By midmorning the King and Mr Churchill appear in the Controller's room. At one stage, Mr Churchill asked if we had any more squadrons to call on? 'No', said the Controller. As the raids die down everyone relaxes at last. Mr Churchill comes down to congratulate the WAAF and RAF on their efforts. Really feel we have earned it! Crawled up those 100 steps to Rest Room feeling 100.

Some City Air Raids: 1940

JOYCE MEEKS SIGNALS RAF CHICKSANDS

Cheadle missed picking up that Coventry was the target for that heavy bombing raid on 14 November, and it was picked up at Folkestone, but not until 3 p.m. – too late for any action to be taken to protect the inhabitants, apart from notification to the Police, Civil-Defence and other services.

VERA COOKE PLOTTER 12 GROUP

I was on duty in the Operations Room when Coventry was bombed. It took a little time to realize what was happening and we had to plot the bombers in, knowing there was nothing we could do personally to stop them.

DORIS NEW BALLOON OPERATOR SITE 79, EDGBASTON

When the morning came, metal splinters could be seen all round the site and we learned that a bomb had dropped in the next street. Many people were killed that night in Birmingham. We counted ourselves lucky that we had suffered no casualties.

During the next day, anti-aircraft guns were placed around the city, in

An exceptionally happy Balloon Site 15 at Llandaff, 1942 (Kathleen Gilkes)

readiness for if there should be any further raid. There was none that night, but the raiders came the following night and were very effectively dealt with, resulting in losses to the Luftwaffe. In all probability, some successes were attributable to our Balloon Barrage, but in order to maintain the secrecy of the weapon attached to our cables, credit was given to the AA gunners!

MARIE WOOD TELEPHONIST RINGWAY (MANCHESTER)/PLYMOUTH

At Ringway I could see my home town ablaze when I was going on night shift. I used to wonder if my parents were OK. I was eventually posted to Plymouth on the first night of the Blitz there. My room-mate was on duty on the switchboard all night. She was only young and her home was in Plymouth, but she didn't utter a murmur but stayed put, all night long. The next time I saw Plymouth it was just rubble and even the local people did not know which street they were walking in. What had been the Guildhall had a banner with just one word, 'Resurgam' [I shall rise again].

SYLVIA SWINBURNE MT FAZACKERLY/PLYMOUTH/BRISTOL/LONDON

Next morning we were horrified to see large pieces of shrapnel all over the camp. A landmine was found near the WAAF quarters, unexploded. That night the Liverpool docks were set on fire, so for the next six nights the bombers had no difficulty in finding their targets and we had no sleep watching the docks burning. Each morning we were relieved to find we were still alive!

On another occasion our station at Bawdsey was being machine-gunned, and I was protected under a table in Plymouth when a nasty air raid took place on the troops being assembled for D-Day. My train from Newquay stopped in Bristol station while the town was being bombed, hardly the safest place to be, and when I arrived at Paddington, all around was being bombed.

The Scharnhorst

VERA ORGAN RADAR BENTLEY PRIORY

I was on duty when the German ship, *Scharnhorst*, steamed out of Brest harbour and was plotted as unidentified shipping through the English Channel until the track was taken over by 11 Group. My link-line operator hinted at panic and error in high places!

MARION MCNEILL   WIRELESS OPERATOR – Y SERVICE (GERMAN LINGUIST)   BEACHY HEAD

I recall the German's message, *Es Schrest Schpitfeure* ['it's snowing Spitfires'] when the three cruisers made their Channel dash.

IRENE CHADNEY   TELEPRINTER OPERATOR   BLETCHLEY PARK (STATION X)

One day we felt that our monotonous existence was all worthwhile, when we had a visit from an RAF Officer – very senior I think, if the scrambled egg on his cap [gold leaves on the peak of the cap] was anything to go by – to tell us that by our efficient handling of messages, the *Scharnhorst* had been sunk!

The Rudolph Hess Flight: May 1941

HELEN HARTNELL   PLOTTER   TURNHOUSE

The Duke of Hamilton was our Commanding Officer when I was posted to Turnhouse. Rudolph Hess, on his historic flight to Scotland in an effort to see the Duke, landed a few miles south of the aerodrome. The station buzzed with rumours, but when I went into Edinburgh that evening the whole place already knew something strange had occurred.

MOLLIE BENNETTO   PLOTTER   KENTON BAR, NEWCASTLE

In the early morning the RDF (Radar) picked up a blip a long way out over the North Sea. We followed it for a while and started a guessing game as to what might be coming at such an unusually fast speed and the straight line it was making towards our coastline. Methodically we plotted co-ordinates, and then it reached the Northumberland shores. Immediately the telephones from the Observer Corps sprang to life: 'Unidentified plane heading north-west. Looks like a Messerschmitt but travelling too fast!' We quickly changed the marker from '?' to 'H' for Hostile.

Well! A plane heading north-west could not be the usual morning information-gathering 'milk run'. Our unidentified plot turned sharply north and then stopped. Silence! We waited desperately for the next sightings. Nothing! No sightings of a wreck or a runaway fugitive or any news!

A few days later, our Group Captain said, 'You remember the disappearing plot? That was the Vice-Chancellor of the German Reich – Rudolph Hess, Hitler's deputy!'

Plotters at work around an Operations Table at Hillingdon (Shelagh Carpenter)

Apparently the great speed of the plane had been possible by stripping
down all unnecessary weight, and the fuel, in the extra tanks that were
added, was practically used up. He had crashed in Scotland. Had he come to
make a private deal for peace with Britain on Hitler's behalf?

The Duke of Kent's Flight: August 1942

JOAN ROBERTSON   CODES AND CYPHERS   INVERGORDON

I was awakened one night to report to the Signals and Meteorological office,
and had to sit receiving various messages regarding a missing plane. This
happened to be the one in which the Duke of Kent was flying to Reykjavik,
Iceland. These were very tense and frustrating hours, as, of course, we could
not believe what had happened, but I know now that I was experiencing a
real touch of Britain's history.

STELLA CRAIG FLYING CONTROL LEUCHARS

> With honour they laid him in the Royal Vault,
> While every head in silent prayer was bent,
> And in the misty Highlands stands a cairn,
> In silent tribute to the Duke of Kent!

Invasion of North Africa: November 1942

SYLVIA SWINBURNE WAAF G ST EVAL

All Officers were called to a special meeting. We were informed that something big was about to happen and all sections were to ensure secrecy at all times. A complete tented camp blossomed and all civilians were removed from the camp for a fortnight.

Imagine my horror when, attending a Church Parade on camp, I heard the preacher talk about the invasion of North Africa. We had not had access to news or radio, so I had not realized what the whole of Britain had been told that morning on the BBC. The Americans had flown in during the night and then taken off for Africa next day to protect our Flying Fortresses.

WINIFRED SMITH PARACHUTE PACKER RINGWAY

We had to go back after our evening meal to work on some special parachutes. These were in beautiful colours – electric blue, red and yellow – each colour to carry some different piece of equipment. We worked till 3 in the morning. Later our WAAF Commanding Officer said that because of our hard work, the Paratroops had their equipment in time and were able to make their first successful landing and take an aerodrome in North Africa. It boosted our morale very much!

Dambuster Raid: May 1943

MARGARET RUSSELL CLERK TYPIST 5 GROUP HEADQUARTERS, GRANTHAM

I typed the Operation Order for the Dambuster Raid. I was locked in the Office and guarded while my typing was checked by the Wing Commander Signals.

GWEN THOMPSON   WIRELESS OPERATOR ACTING AS TELEPHONIST   SCAMPTON

I was on the switchboard that night. There was all this activity – we just thought it was practice, but when they asked for 'The White House, Washington', we realized something big was happening. Then we saw all this gold braid coming into the Signals Section and Bomber Harris was there!

I was also in the Signals Section when they had to send out fifty-six telegrams for all the aircrew who were missing on that raid!

The Invasion of Sicily: July 1943

DOROTHY OSBON   EQUIPMENT ASSISTANT   ST ATHAN

One day a man came from Air Ministry. The station had been building up its holding of vehicles. The man said to me, 'Think! Those vehicles are going to land on sand!' From this I realized that normal road-tread tyres would be no use. So I put my orders in for special tyres and I went to Cardiff with this gentleman to pick them up. All the odd things I wanted, I could demand, with no forms or formalities. He just signed.

At work in Air Intelligence at Headquarters Coastal Command, Northwood, 1944 (Patricia Lloyd-Lawrence)

Later I found this was for the invasion of Sicily for use by the Argyll and Sutherland Highlanders.

Peenemunde Raid: August 1943

MONICA HUGHES   CLERK   MEDMENHAM

There were members of all the services based here, which made for a very good atmosphere. I was there when the V2 rocket site was pinpointed on our photographs, and we had press photographers in. Somewhere in the archives might be a photo of me, or rather a photo of just my hands!

JOAN DINGWALL   RADAR OPERATOR   BAWDSEY

Our WAAF Sergeant came into the Ops Room one day to announce that the several hundred planes we had previously tracked had been on a raid to

Airwomen working in the Radar Operations Room at Bawdsey, 1944. The Radar screen is concealed for secrecy (Joan Dingwall, Denise Wynn, Elaine Dew)

Peenemunde – the German rocket establishment – and that it had been almost totally destroyed.

A German Spy

WINKIE LOUGHRAN WIRELESS OPERATOR ISLE OF ISLAY, SCOTLAND

I relayed ranges and details of aircraft in code to Castlerock, Northern Ireland, from Saligo Bay.

One day, while I was 'working' Ireland on our secret frequency, I was interrupted by an unknown sender. I managed to keep him sending, by telling him, in our international morse, 'I can't hear well. Keep sending'. Meanwhile, our boss of the watch got a station down the coast to try and locate his position. Several days later the station notified us that he had been found, and proved to be a German spy with a wireless set out on a point of land off the coast of Ireland!

Corona

AIR VICE-MARSHAL ADDISON RADAR COUNTER MEASURES AIR MINISTRY

We picked up enemy signals and retransmitted them, so confusing the Luftwaffe pilot that he did not know whether he was listening to his or ours. When he tried to get a bearing, we gave him one! We gave him false weather reports and directions. I have heard German aircraft over London being told they were over Peterborough!

RUTH ORNSTEIN Y SERVICE (GERMAN LINGUIST) WEST KINGSDOWN, KENT

24 July 1944 Ruth to German pilot '. . . *das war die feind stimme – ich bin eure grundstation*'. ['. . . that was the enemy's voice. *I* am your ground station'.]
24 July 1944 – The pilot of a Junkers 88 landed at Bembridge, Isle of Wight. He *said* he had wireless telegraphy failure and had mistaken the Bristol Channel for the English Channel!

Churchill: Conferences

JOAN LLEWELLYN CODE AND CYPHER OFFICER CABINET OFFICE CYPHER OFFICE

At the time of Churchill's illness in the Middle East, I took a number of

Cypher Officers to help in North Africa. Four of our party went to Tunis to work for the Prime Minister at Carthage until he was well enough to fly to Marrakesh, where I had already set up the Cypher Office in the lodge of the Taylor villa, where Churchill was to recuperate.

I also took some Cypher Officers to the 1944 Quebec Conference and some were present at the Yalta and Potsdam Conferences, as well as the Cripps Mission to India.

JEAN HALE   CODE AND CYPHER OFFICER   CABINET OFFICE CYPHER OFFICE

When Mr Churchill became ill [rumoured to have suffered a heart attack] after the November 1943 Teheran Conference, it was decided to fly half our Officers out to Marrakesh to deal with the telegrams for the War Office, the remaining half stayed in London to receive them. I was lucky enough to go.

HILDA BELL   FLIGHT MECHANIC – ENGINES   HOLMSLEY SOUTH

We got aircraft ready for quite a number of things – VIP trips to Italy, and Mr Churchill and Mr Eden's planes ready for their trip to Yalta. I worked on the York aircraft on which Mr Churchill's pilot perfected his flying. He did

A Flight Mechanic with her aircraft at Spitalgate, 1945 (Phyllis Moore)

landings and circuits and bumps, as well as trying out anything that *might* happen, so that he would know what to do!'

Experiments

Station Camouflage

HAZEL WILLIAMS PLOTTER

I tried to get into the RAF at 14½ with my grandfather, he subtracting and me adding to my age. I did make it at 17½ and he got to be in charge of a 'Starfish' site at 72! These were decoy buildings set alight to look like burning towns, to fool the German bombers to unload their bombs.

STELLA BUIST FLYING CONTROL LEUCHARS

One day somebody thought of a brilliant idea to camouflage the airfield. Hedges were painted across the runways, to create the impression that we were really a couple of farms. We thought no pilot would be hoodwinked into thinking we were anything but an aerodrome! However, an aircraft from another station arrived one day and to our surprise kept circling us. Eventually he did come in to land, and when we enquired into his strange hesitation, the pilot said, 'Your airfield is so well camouflaged, I couldn't find the damned runway!'

Fido

MARGARET CULVERHOUSE METEOROLOGIST RAF MELBOURNE

14 Feb 1943 – 'Woke to find deep snow. Very cold in hut. On day shift, 8 a.m. to 5 p.m. No operations as they are installing FIDO [Fog Intensification Dispersal Operations], which is to be tested next week [oil fires to counter poor visibility for landing aircraft]. One of us has to cycle down the runway holding an anemometer – I hope it isn't me! (It was!)

DAPHNE LIGHT MT FINMERE

Because of the fog in Lincolnshire, a number of Lancasters had been diverted to us and FIDO was in operation. The smell of burning oil, the smoke and the heavies circling overhead was a dramatic sight. I was driving the ambulance, waiting for casualties.

Window

Window consisted of thousands of little strips of silver foil, each metal object giving a trace on enemy Radar screens, which could be a plane. It was part of Radar Counter Measures (RCM).

DAPHNE ALLISON   RADAR MECHANIC   NEVIN

An experiment in Radar jamming – window – was carried out while I was here. The results were negative and no one could understand why. It was then discovered that the window had not been scattered, but dropped tied up in solid bales. Luckily the only casualty was a cow, hit by a descending bale! [A later experiment even misled the RAF into believing it had to counter thousands of German aircraft in the north.]

Jet Engine

HOLLY I'ANSON   FLYING CONTROL   LANCASTER SQUADRON

I was stationed on Lancaster Squadrons during the 1,000 bomber raids and had an interesting spell working in co-operation with the Meteor Test Pilots, when Frank Whittle's jet aircraft was still on the secret list.

DORA HATCH   CLERK   BOSCOMBE DOWN

On 18 April 1944 we had a new aircraft delivered to the Flight. The shape was unconventional and the noise, when the engines were turned on, was unlike anything I had previously heard. It was, in fact, an early jet aircraft – DH E6/41, and on 22 April it was given its first Test Flight by Group Captain Purvis.

Pluto

KAY BALL   RADIOGRAPHER   RAF HOSPITAL, MELKSHAM

I was given orders, a little while before D-Day, to set up my X-ray

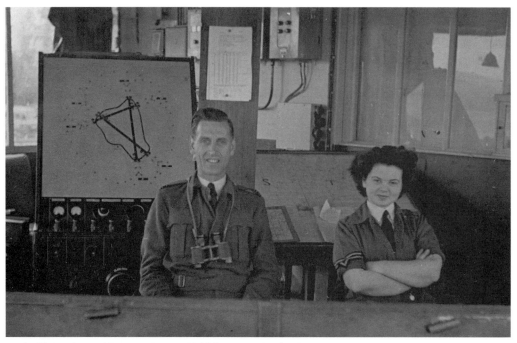

In the Flying Control Tower at Exeter, 1945 (Margaret Trickett)

department for screening. A group of about four well-dressed civilian men arrived, carrying concealed what looked to me like a length of rubber piping. I couldn't think what on earth they wanted to screen *that* for. I was made to understand it was a top security project and very hush hush.

It was not revealed to me what it was until well after D-Day. The men were interested to see how the joints were connecting in the lengths of rubber tubing. It turned out to be one of the Avon Rubber Works' wartime products, PLUTO, the famous pipeline that was laid between England and France to take the essential petrol for the vehicles of the invasion forces!

Penicillin

JOAN SMYTH   DISPENSER   RAF HOSPITAL, HALTON

In 1944 I was involved in preparing ampoules of the new drug, penicillin. At this time its injection was so painful that it was given in conjunction with a local anaesthetic, but so effective that daily batches were being sent from Halton to medical units of the Second Front!

RAF hospital staff, Melksham, 1944 (Kathleen Ball)

Helicopter

EVE HALL   CLERK ACCOUNTS   MANBY

Once, returning to the building with two mugs of NAAFI tea, I heard a
terrific noise. I looked above and saw this monster flying towards me, very
low. I was petrified, thinking it might be a doodle-bug or such. I then
realized that I was looking at my first helicopter in flight.

MRS TAYLOR   FABRIC WORKER   ANDOVER

With another airman from the Fabric Section, I was sent to do a 'special
job'. We always worked well together, myself being the only WAAF at that
particular time, on the strength of the station workshops.

  We were allotted a hangar and told to clear it out and keep all dust to a
minimum. After nearly a week some people from Air Ministry, along with
more Officers, including, I think, two Americans, came. The Americans told

us what the job was to be. It was to make a cover for the new American Sikorski helicopter – the plane to be delivered next day. Nobody in the United Kingdom had seen one before!

No one, except the two of us, was allowed into the hangar. We studied the existing cover and made loads of sketches and notes, and then, feeling extremely nervous, we started to take it to pieces. All the materials we needed were delivered and several pairs of gloves in white.

Every piece we took off, we laid out on the floor and made patterns of each section. There were numerous zip-fasteners of very heavy metal to be measured and written into the pattern. In fact, every little mark we made a note of.

The big moment came when we undid the material sent to us to do the job. It was called Medapolin – a very fine, lovely white material, so soft, and just like a good quality hanky cloth, similar to a fine cambric. We looked at the zips and could see loads of problems, for some of them had to be sewn in a circle. However, we ploughed on with the cutting. I was too nervous, so I left this to my partner. I did the drawing and nearly all the sewing, including those dreadful heavy zips.

Once we had made the cover, we said a few prayers that it would fit and on the first time of trying, it fitted like a glove! We finished about 3 in the afternoon. Everyone agreed on the fit and when the place was cleared of spectators, we set about the task of getting the finish ready. We were not too troubled in painting the cover with the final coat, as this was only the camouflage and markings. Then we cleared everything into the side rooms, sprayed the hanger with a hose, and were proud to report to our very jolly Warrant Officer, that the work was complete.

The real joy came when the doors were opened. We were so very proud of our work!

7
D-DAY, JUNE 1944

My heart goes out in admiration and my voice in prayer,
To the fellows who have dared to storm the beaches over there;
To the ships that took them over and the men who cleared the mines,
To the gliders and the Paratroops who dropped behind the lines.
Of their daring and their courage, I could shout and sing aloud;
My heart goes out in admiration and my heart is proud!

Kathleen Partridge

D-Day, under the code-name Operation Overlord, was the re-entry into Europe
of Allied personnel. It is remembered by the Veterans of today for many things. It
served, partly, as a superb example of meticulous planning and co-ordinated effort
by a huge mixed group of fourteen Allied nations; but, above all, D-Day stands as
a memorial to the battles to help free Europe from German occupation, in which
many people gave their lives for this freedom. It was not the end of this ferocious
war, but it was certainly the beginning of the end!

Such a vast enterprise could not be hidden from the eyes of service personnel
or civilian alike, even those least involved, and in the Forces women played a large
part in the preparations.

The following extracts describe D-Day as seen through the eyes of WAAF,
many of whom had walked around with the knowledge, tucked away in their
secret minds, for as long as six months beforehand. Indeed, they had suspected it
might have happened in 1943, as it had, in fact, been intended!

Before D-Day

CATRIN MARTIN RADIO TELEPHONY OPERATOR MANSTON

We knew for several weeks that something was on the cards, as all leave had
been cancelled for about eight weeks, although that had happened in 1943
for about four weeks.

SYLVIA WALKER   RADAR OPERATOR   TANNACH AND ULBSTER, SCOTLAND

In early 1944 I was plotting shipping off the north-east coast of Scotland. Suddenly it seemed we were tracking large numbers of ships coming out of the naval base in the Orkneys and going south, south!

PAT EVANS   RADAR OPERATOR   BRANDY BAY, DORSET

Tyneham village was evacuated later in the war and used as a gunnery range by the Tank Corps at Lulworth. The lovely Elizabethan manor house, where we had lived, is now simply a shell, and the rows of cottages in the dear little fishing village are just ruins.

[Pat's friend, Ann Welch, thinks the village was used to practise invasion and landings.]

JOYCE BARRETT   CLERK   RAF RECORDS

Later in the war I remember an all-night cider party at an American camp. It was beautifully warm weather. We linked arms and walked through flower-filled meadows and sang all the songs of the deep south. Next day there was a great rumbling of trucks and we were left with the wind of their passing. We never saw them again.

Radar Operators off duty in Warborrow Bay, Tyneham, 1943 (Pat Evans)

MAVIS PICKFORD RADAR UXBRIDGE

Just before D-Day, the grassy areas of the camp gradually sprouted numerous tents and we became conscious of a sudden influx of male personnel including those of the Allies. Also the town filled up with Americans who very soon made friends with 'the little Waafys'. On one occasion they sent transport for a dance. They showered us with American cigarettes and chocolate (they said they had more than they needed) and for the first time in many years we tasted ice-cream – it even had bits of fruit in it! But by the middle of June 1944 the camp was suddenly back to normal and the town strangely quiet once more.

JOAN DINGWALL RADAR OPERATOR PEVENSEY

6 May 1944 – Took bus to Eastbourne. Every field, country lane and farmyard is crammed with military vehicles and equipment – tanks, guns, the lot! Nice warm sunny afternoon, so decided to have a look at the sea. Bit dangerous! The beach is mined, a barricade of iron stakes are right along the sands and rolls of thick barbed wire all along the top of the promenade. Across the road the hotels are almost derelict – windows boarded up, front walls down, roofs gone. Big gap filled with Army lorries. The Army seems to have occupied any habitable building.

'An American asked to have some photos with a WAAF to send back home', April 1944 (Kay Moore)

KATHLEEN JOHNSON   FLIGHT MECHANIC   LINCOLN

Belonging to a work gang consisting of WAAF and RAF, we worked on the
Horsa and Waco gliders which took part in the invasion. We were three
weeks confined to camp and worked around the clock, modifying the gliders
in a hangar. The men did not have time to shave, and we wore battledress,
overalls and men's boots. What a sight we must have looked!

ELIZABETH WOODIN   CLERK   UXBRIDGE

I remember typing lots of stencils for Operation Overlord, and every item I
typed was preceded by D+ and a figure. Little did I know that I was typing the
phasing-in instructions for the group's aircraft and equipment to go onto the
Continent after D-Day! For security reasons these stencils had to be locked
away each night, and the safe place was just a wooden stationery cupboard!

The Day Before

The weather for the appointed day of 5 June 1944 turned mutinous, with driving
rain and gale-force winds that lashed the sea to fury. Many of the craft, already
filled with waiting men, were awash with sea water and vomit, and the crossing
was aborted. On that same day, with a meteorological forecast of a short next-day
improvement, General Eisenhower, Supreme Commander of the Allied
Expeditionary Force, decided, 'Okay . . . We'll go'. These words set in motion
the greatest invasion Europe had ever known.

Overnight came the airborne assault on key inland positions; when the Paratroops
from the gliders had landed, the ships began their voyage across the Channel, starting
their landings on the five beaches of Normandy in the early hours of 6 June.

The Night Before

SHEILA FOWLER   TELEPRINTER OPERATOR   HILLINGDON

The Sector Commanders came to Hillingdon just before D-Day for briefing,
and then a few nights later I took the signal down to the Controller, stating
that Operation Overlord would commence in the morning.

EILEEN BASSETT   METEOROLOGIST   FELIXSTOWE

I was cooking sausages on toast for my night duty supper, when the Tannoy
burst into voice. 'This is D-Day. Not a practice. This is D-Day.'

Met. airwomen consulting the latest weather map in the Meteorological Office at Spitalgate, summer 1945 (Irene Park)

The outer door of the Met. Office flew open and our Station Commander rushed in and made for the Forecast Office, where, to the increasing smell of burning toast, I pointed out the salient features of the weather chart. We had seen many preparations for the invasion, but the idea had not been real until now!

As the Commanding Officer departed, the first heavy transports could be heard rolling along the Langer Road towards the naval gate, where they would turn into camp and wait in ranks on the hards for embarkation. During the cover of darkness, the great Tank Loading Craft had manoeuvred into position by our old gantries, up till now unused to much greater activity than lifting the occasional flying boat out of the water for maintenance.

PAT SPARKS PLOTTER SOPLEY

Just going out when the CO came in and put me in charge, not to let anyone out and any returning airwomen to stay in billet. Also to go on duty one hour earlier.

We all went on duty at 10 p.m. A talk by CO to say, 'This is the day – D-Day!' Worked extremely hard all night and prayed for all those boys out in the Channel – so many friends!

D-Day Itself: 6 June 1944

At dawn we hear gunfire [Pat Sparks continues] and are allowed on to the roof for a few minutes to see the gun flares.

Very tired after night duty and so straight to bed. Woken at noon by the Cooks who tell us the invasion has started. What were we doing all night? The busiest and most thrilling time of my life!

ALICE NEIGHBOUR   FLIGHT MECHANIC   WING

Duty airwoman brings in a jug of hot cocoa from the Cookhouse. An air of excitement as rumours of D-Day abound. Usual everyday chores. Cycle to main camp for breakfast and then on to the airfield and hangars. By now we know that D-Day has begun. Usual work on the aircraft in the hangar, but with the added excitement of some tactical airforce landing through damage. Asked one pilot what it was like over there? 'Bloody Marvellous! You feel you couldn't get a pin between the ships.' Worked through the day, but followed the radio news bulletins intently.

ELIZABETH ANDREWS   RADAR OPERATOR   BEACHY HEAD

0600 hours. On duty on the T16 (Radar). Omaha Beach taking a battering. Andy is there – Combined Operations – attached to the 1st or 9th Americans. 21 BDU taken off the Invasion Board – all lost! (Fortunately he was one of the few survivors but was wounded. Those who could walk were helped off the beach at about 1600 hours by the C of E Padre)

JOYCE MOLLETT   PLOTTER   MIDDLE WALLOP

The work was very front line and very secret, suffice it to say that I spent the whole of the morning of D-Day plotting convoys, and I remember the thrill when a voice called out, 'We're in contact with France, sir!'

DORIS MURRAY   CODE AND CYPHERS   HEADQUARTERS COASTAL COMMAND

My most exciting 24 hours, beginning with the anticipation, then the decyphering of D-Day Signals and finally at the end of the watch, going out of the underground office and seeing the aircraft with their invasion markings going overhead!

PRIMROSE SKINNER TELEPHONIST UXBRIDGE

I was due to be on duty at 1300 hrs, and during the morning the sky was black with our planes going over to Normandy.

Decoy Invasion

On the night of 5 June 105 RAF planes and 34 Royal Navy small ships took part in diversionary manoeuvres which were code-named Taxable, ABC Patrol, Glimmer, Mandrel and Titanic. Covering the real landings, they were to draw the German defence forces to the wrong areas. They succeeded admirably.

JOSEPHINE GOLDIE-SCOT RADAR OPERATOR ST MARGARET'S BAY

In the early hours the long-anticipated invasion of France looked as though it might be starting as the PPI (Radar) got busier and busier. During my free hour about dawn, I stood outside and watched the long trail of craft passing close in, on their way across the Channel.

It seems that our invasion was a sort of decoy, and that the real invasion was further along the coast from Portsmouth to the Normandy coast, where they have made a floating harbour [Mulberry]. A lot of casualties, I'm afraid!

D-Day and the Aftermath

KAY BALL RADIOGRAPHER RAF HOSPITAL, MELKSHAM

In the early hours of D-Day I was called out to X-ray an Army pilot who had several shrapnel wounds in his legs. At the end of that morning I received a message to say I had to get my small kit packed for 2 p.m., when a staff car would pick me up to take me to RAF hospital, Wroughton.

On arriving there I saw the hospital grounds were full of tents, for extra staff posted in to receive casualties. Within a few hours the first siren alerted us that casualties had arrived by plane at Lyneham, flown from the beaches of Normandy, where medics had given first aid. A fleet of ambulances brought them from the planes and they were wheeled into the hutted structure built for the purpose, where eight Medical Officers examined them and put big labels on them as to what treatment they were to receive, such as blood transfusions, X-rays, resuscitation or surgery. The stretchers were pushed by German Prisoners of War to the right department. It was a wonderful system with only a few cases of gangrene, owing to the swiftness of the evacuation.

We had eight X-ray tables going at once. Some days we worked as long as ten to fourteen hours. The prisoners brought us sandwiches and tea, which we consumed as we worked. When the all-clear went, meaning the flights had finished, we would go to bed, whatever time it was.

From the X-ray department the casualties would be moved on to a side ward for the Preparation Room and then to the Theatre, where as many as eight operating tables would be used by surgeons all the time. Then the casualties passed to the ordinary wards. Next day, ambulances would take all but the very ill to hospitals all over the country, leaving our hospital ready to take the next influx of casualties.

The Following Days

EILEEN BASSETT   METEOROLOGIST   FELIXSTOWE

During the following days, history was unrolling under our eyes! But Pearl and I, locked into camp during that eventful night duty (to cover 24 hours

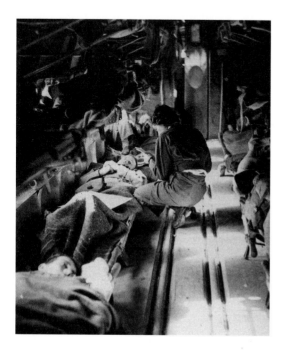

WAAF Nursing Orderly on an Air Ambulance Dakota, tending stretcher cases evacuated from France in June 1944 (Joan Crane)

until the rest of the staff could be let in) found life too hectic to appreciate it. All through those heady days and nights, the heavy transports, ambulances with Royal Army Medical Corps personnel and snorting amphibious tanks rolled on through the gate and eventually were loaded into the huge gaping jaws of the Tank Loading Craft. We kept the kettle boiling continuously, so that when the Royal Marine Officers came in, wet and weary, for their hourly forecasts, we could shove hot mugs of tea into their grateful hands.

The weather turned sour and on one frightful day a treacherous gust of wind carried the bows of one of the Tank Loading Craft across the gantry, and the whole ship had to be unloaded, the men working up to their waists in water, most untypically cold for June!

Arnhem: September 1944

IRENE FROWEN   DENTAL ORDERLY   TARRANT RUSHTON

17–18 September – The Tannoy going all the time. Airlift going on. Walked the mile to Sick Quarters, past aircraft and gliders all lined up. Appointments for dental treatment not kept by one individual. Today they went to Arnhem!

Flight Mechanics and MT girls in the hut all had the same thing to tell. We kept on listening to the radio. The station was still sealed, waiting for the next lift to go. Not an easily forgotten day!

JEAN YOUNG   RADAR OPERATOR   BARKWAY

17 September – Almost like another D-Day. Allied troops landed in three places in Holland.

27 September – After listening to the news all week for news about the 2nd Army's unsuccessful attempts to relieve our airborne division at Arnhem, a security ban put on. Tonight the full story was told. The remnants of the division were withdrawn on Monday night, but of 7,000 men, only 2,000 were brought back and 1,500 wounded were left behind with the Royal Army Medical Corps. They must have had a terrible time, under fire continuously for nine days and nights – food, water and ammunition run out.

WINIFRED SMITH   PARACHUTE PACKER   RINGWAY

All our pilots had bad injuries, perhaps a leg missing or something, but they still wanted to fly! They were good pilots – they had to be – we couldn't afford

A Dakota passing over Biggin Hill on its return from Arnhem, September 1944 (Vera Storkey)

to have our Paratroops killed! I think when it came to Arnhem, these were the ones who flew their planes over there. Our instructors went as despatchers.

One was lucky that he was able to walk out with the few troops that were left, after fighting with them. He was the only doctor able to walk, to help with the walking wounded, and became my family doctor here in Christchurch (New Zealand). He was a Scot with black hair, but he walked out an old man with white hair!

Afterwards

MAUREEN SUTTON PAY CLERK CLIFTON, YORK

I joined this Unit Base Accounts for all the Air Force personnel involved in the D-Day Landings, where I was able to follow the course of the war by all the different currencies that they were paid in!

8
THE DAILY ROUND

When the WAAF was formed on 28 June 1939, its 1,734 members were already enrolled in six types of work: Cooks, Clerks, Mess Orderlies, MT Drivers, Equipment Assistants and, on Balloon Squadrons, Fabric Workers – all under the aegis of the RAF companies of the Auxiliary Territorial Service. The companies were supposed to have sixty-seven women each, with five more if they had Fabric Workers, but not all companies were up to full strength.

WAAF March Past King George VI, Queen Elizabeth and Mary, the Queen Mother, at the National Defence Rally of all Women's Services in Hyde Park, 2 July 1939. This was the first wearing of the WAAF uniform in public, four days after the WAAF was formed (Lesley Nightingale)

One of the most obvious trades was Clerk, since airwomen were there to release airmen for first-line duties. However, remnants of the past still lingered as Margaret Furness was to discover: 'Some Commanding Officers required you to take shorthand, standing to attention!' But others were treated in a more friendly manner, like Dilys Upton at Avening Court in Gloucester, the Base Personnel Staff Office: 'Our Flight Sergeant was a good sport. He let us imprison him between the huge windows and the blackout curtains. When our unit moved to Clifton, York, we managed to get him into a packing crate and then we sat on it!' Obviously, he was too good to lose!

An intriguing and memory-nudging ode, sent by Jackie Poulton and composed by her course at Kirkham in July 1944, exhibits the variety of RAF forms with which Clerks General Duties had to contend – as well as the ordinary airman or airwoman!

I must have used a lot of forms,
Yet having no idea,
That had I cared to glance, I'd find
A number printed there.
If someone named a 575
It wouldn't mean a thing,
Yet often to the cobbler my
Down-trodden shoes I bring.
Form 292 I know quite well
From last year's course PT,
I little thought, 'Result of Course'
Could mean so much to me.
And quite soon now Form 413
Will take me on my way,
Back to Record Office, Gloucester,
But not for long I pray.
I'm hoping that Appendix B
For Raf 1020A,
Will be the means of moving me
To better things someday.
Then filling in Forms 381 –
The Record Card of Leave –

I'll thank the Clk/GD course for
The numbers up my sleeve!
I'll never use a 252
I hope, but if I can,
I'll hand out heaps of 295s
To every girl or man.
And so until that special form
That's 1394,
Close up the AP 837,
For forms won't win the war!
1672s in plenty,
And RB 12 and 8,
Would help to pass the time away
In very pleasant state.
We hope that someday soon we'll raise
Form 1755,
And bury all these books and forms,
Which cause us all to strive
So hard to reach the standard, that's
Required to suit the Raf,
And be a perfect Clk/GD,
While serving in the WAAF!

KEY
Form: 575   Shoe Repair Label
       292   Result of Course
       413   Railway Warrant
       Appendix B   Application for Commission (WAAF)
       1020A   Application for Commission (RAF)
       381   Record of Leave (Officers)
       252   Charge Form
       295   Leave and Pass Form
       1394   Certificate of Discharge
       1672   Railway Warrant and Leave Form
       1755   Burial Certificate
       RB 12 & 8   Ration Cards

The work of an Equipment Assistant, another of the early trades, was not all plain sailing either. Men and girls usually worked in huge premises, crowded with tall racks which were filled with a vast variety of goods, each with its own name and number, which had to be recorded and recognized. Here the area most familiar to ordinary airwomen was the Clothing Store, packed with items of uniform.

'Cupboards 20 ft high' (specially drawn by David Langdon from 1941 original)

However, not all Equipment work was as stereotyped. On her first posting to
Middle Wallop (then a night-fighter station), Joyce McKay was 'the disher out of
petrol, both MT and aviation, a job that I loved, in spite of the exposure to weather
– or perhaps because of it! I was always known as 'Stinker' – as my surname was
then Murdoch – but no doubt it was only too suitable, because of my job!'

In 1943 Vera Crow found herself on 'a rather unusual posting, as I was the only
WAAF among 28,000 RAF when I was posted on Equipment to the RAF
Airfield Construction Service.'

Sometimes the men could be very cruel to girls who found their work hard.
Both Betty Ingle on Equipment and Bertha Pepper, a cook, encountered some
men who said, 'You joined to do a man's job. Do it!' So they did!

Driver MT, translated variously as either Motor, Mechanical or Military
Transport, was always very popular and airwomen who joined to do this were
often disappointed and ended up doing something different because the trade was
full. Drivers drove most kinds of transport, including mortuary and pig-swill vans
and anything up to 3 tons, with often no training at all!

One of the lucky ones was Margaret Green:

The reaction of most men to us was helpful, especially a rather battered ex-
boxer, nicknamed 'Tiger' Tasker ('the Bolton Terror' turned MT Mechanic),
who when I said I was scared to take the Commer for the first time through
the Bar at Beverley, volunteered to accompany me on his off-duty time!

In Beverley a WAAF driving a truck hit a market stall of fruit, which was
scattered in all directions, but she was so gentle and apologetic in her
demeanour that she was given an apple and told to be on her way. Later the
same driver in a fog hit a cow on the stray. The cow got up and wandered
off, the Commer had to be towed in!

A number of incidents happened to Phyllis Cove, in the course of her work:

On one occasion I was detailed to take an aircrew to start their operations on
a certain wartime aerodrome, flying Stirling bombers. On arrival, the
Guardroom told me to take them and their kit to Hut 13. After unloading
and checking out, I returned to my home base.

A week later – the same kind of detail – another crew and kit to go to the
same operational aerodrome. On checking with the Guardroom, I was told

Driver and friends on an MT 3-ton Dodge in convoy, Conway, 1944 (Cherry Symonds)

to take them to Hut 13 – again! Evidently my first crew had never returned from one of their operations. Saying nothing to this crew, I deposited them and their kit, and then left. Many weeks later I was again detailed to take yet another crew to the same place. Checking in with the Guardroom, I was informed that Hut 14 was their destination, but afterwards, on checking out at the Guardroom, I told the Military Policeman that I was sure it was the same hut to which I had previously taken the two crews. He told me that the second crew were reported missing on their operations. As aircrew were a superstitious lot, Hut 13 had been turned into 14!

Many months later, I was pleased to hear that my third crew had completed their tour and moved on!

Another time three Officers were detailed to judge a baby competition. That in itself was a laugh – none had any family, and two were single. What they knew about babies, you could have written on a matchbox. While I was driving the staff car to Norfolk, these three decided to rope me in to help them. They hadn't a clue, but neither did I!

Anyway, on our arrival we were placed on a dais, while on the floor of the Social Hall (what a misnomer!) were the mothers with their shrieking babies! Above the din it was quite an education to listen to the Officers' remarks. If they fancied the mother's looks, the baby was in the running. I rather think I put a block on a lot of their ideas!

Yet another job was to take a refuse lorry – an old Dennis – to a dump about seven miles away. This lorry had a gatecrash gearbox (no synchromesh in those days). A Dennis was always a disaster for anyone driving it. To get to the driving seat, you had to step onto the big front wheel on top of the mudguard, and when you were up there you could see over all the hedges! It was cumbersome and unwieldy!

Well! I approached the main road through the village, thinking to myself that it seemed to be behaving well! But there was some Army traffic coming through the other way, so I had to change down the gearbox. With this old lorry it meant that you brought her out of gear, listened to the engine, then double-declutching, shoved it into lower gear. Gosh, did I miscalculate! You have never heard such a grinding and clashing of gears! Heads turned and mortification set in. If there had been a hole in the road, I'd have cheerfully jumped in.

Anyway, I finally made it and duly arrived at the refuse dump. It was situated in a very narrow lane, with a small opening to take a lorry. The RAF chap who worked there said to me, 'Back the lorry in'. My heart sank! I knew he expected me to mess it up. I swung the lorry round, reversed it in, with a few inches to spare on either side, and jumped down. The RAF fellow said, 'For a girl you did damn well! Most of the RAF Drivers break the hedges down.' Drawing myself haughtily upwards and with an icy look I said, 'WAAF Drivers aren't all bad, you know!'

Monica Dunbar, another WAAF Driver, had an unusual tale to tell:

While I was waiting beside my staff car, I saw Mr MacIndoe, the famous plastic surgeon, standing a little way off. I had driven him, maybe twice, at the beginning of the war. To my surprise, he came over and asked me how I was? I was astonished. 'Sir,' I said, 'You amaze me. How can you possibly remember me after so long?' With a delightful smile he answered, 'That's my job, to remember faces. One day I might have to remake yours.' He repaired many a burned and shattered face of mutilated aircrew when their planes went on fire.'

MT Mechanics did not appear until sometime later, to the annoyance of some men, like Ada Ryder's Station Commander, who in any case seemed to hate all WAAF!

There were only two of us at Manby and we were the first there. One day the Commanding Officer detailed me to service his own car. It had lain there since 1939, and this was 1943! The Warrant Officer took me to the CO's house, outside the camp, and into his garage. I lifted the bonnet. 'No,' said the Station Warrant Officer. 'He wants the interior doing first.' So I opened the doors, half got in and lifted the seats. Gosh! I don't know who was the more frightened! Thousands of mice jumped out at me. They'd been nesting there since 1939!

The Commanding Officer, Group Captain Ivens, knew it and wanted to teach the WAAF a lesson, the old devil! He wasn't called 'Ivan the Terrible' for nothing! I just left everything, and ran hell for leather back to the MT yard. Afterwards I kept well out of his way, and I was there for two-and-a-half years!

There were, in addition, two much-overworked early trades of Kitchen Orderlies and Cooks, who in the beginning often went straight from preparing meals for a small family to supplying the needs of hundreds or even thousands! Life could be far from uneventful!

While on duty one day at St Athan, Eileen Slawson heard there had been

a breakout of German Prisoners of War from Farm Island Camp, near Bridgend. I was preparing early morning breakfast, when a noise from the empty Dining Hall frightened the helper and myself. Plucking up courage, I went to investigate, and found a man in RAF uniform banging on one of the tables. I could not understand his reply to my question, and I immediately suspected that he was an escaped prisoner, who had somehow obtained a uniform. I brought him a mug of tea and some food, while I contacted the Service Police.

I was elated that I had helped capture an escaped German, but was completely deflated, when, about an hour later, I was told he was a drunk Irishman, who had been celebrating St Patrick's Day!

Having done pre-RAF training for Cordon Bleu, Pamela Crump chose to be a Cook.

Cooks in the Airmen's Mess, Hucknall, 1939 (Daisy Hills)

We were the first airwomen to go to the RAF Halton School of Cookery, and the men we were with seemed to think that if we used a large knife we would cut ourselves, and that we always needed a chair to sit on. We learned to cook for hundreds.

Later, after promotion, a Wing Commander Flying interviewed me at Wellesbourne. He had never had a WAAF Catering Officer before, and just did not know what to say. Eventually, having become very red-faced, he asked me if I could stir porridge!

Three days after the war began, the trade of Codes and Cyphers appeared and those who were chosen bore very heavy and secret responsibilities. Messages in code or cypher came through Joan McAdam's office. 'Convoys of ships in the Atlantic all had code-names, such "Penguin" or "Child" etc. They were given air protection on the most vulnerable part of their route, from the dangers of German submarines. On reaching the convoy, the pilot would send back a message, "Am

Code and Cypher Officer en route for Egypt, August 1941 (Doreen Morle)

with" and the code-name of the convoy. On this particular day the message received was simply "Pregnant!"'

WAAF Nurses appeared in 1940 and gradually divided into different specializations. They were not, however, normally employed in the same way as Bonney Budd: 'While at Hinton-in-the-Hedges, in 1943, the Station Medical Officer and I attended the lying-in of the station sow. My father being a pig man, I was able to advise the MO. The litter, when older, broke out and knocked the Adjutant off his cycle, causing him to be treated at Station Sick Quarters. Meanwhile a Tannoy was sent out for all station personnel to turn out and round up their Christmas dinner!' Bonney also notes, in another peculiarity of RAF jargon, that station ambulances were called irreverently, 'Blood Tubs'.

'Wellesbourne was an Operational Training Unit (OTU) and there were a lot of crashes', says Louie McGaughey.

The men would take the ambulance, while we nurses prepared the crash room and beds. Most of the time though, it was very smashed up bodies they brought back, sometimes so badly burned they were hardly recognizable as human beings. We WAAF had to help in the mortuary and it was a terrifying experience. The first time I was sent to help I was nineteen, and I thought I would die before I got out of there again, but I managed to go through with it. Once, I found that one of the bodies was a boy I had been out with a couple of nights before. They were all so young – late teens and early twenties.

Barbara McMaster has one particular memory of 'when a Lancaster bomber crashed on Croydon airport. All the crew were killed except two. We left our supper to drag them out. Then we nursed the two survivors back to full health.' Later in Croydon's Sick Quarters at Peaks Hill, Purley, she recalls:

When the doodle-bugs started, everyone at Peaks Hill fled to a shelter down the garden. Bombs we understood, but these black monsters trailing fire only to cut out diving earthwards seemed apparitions of Satan. We looked at each other in fear. Then I remembered Joan. We had left her in bed, immobile, so I went back. We sat in the dark, holding hands. 'Please God, let me live till morning,' muttered Joan. 'Yes,' I echoed fervently. In all my wartime

Photographers with developing tank and drier. Benson, 1945 (Eileen Jacobs)

experience, I have never felt so frozen as I felt that night. It was stifling in the room, but Joan and I shivered the long hours away.

In the opinion of Marguerite Auton, 'work as a Dental Hygienist was hard, and cleaning the surgery floor every day, tiring. The working in and rolling of mercury on the palms of our hands was injurious, being absorbed by the body, eventually affecting health. Today it is all done by machinery.'

When photographer Stella Adams reported to Farnborough, 'the gate sent me to Station Headquarters, since, "There are no WAAF Photographers at the School of Photography!" When I eventually arrived at my new posting, I was blasted out for being late!'

Near the end of the war it was Betty Trull's luck as a photographer to use 'the new colour film called Kodachrome on the F24s. Then comes the long wait for the first Lancasters to return. We start processing the film about 2200 hours. For the first time we can see the bomb damage and fires in colour. I look at it in wonder. The colours are like jewels. Then I take it to Intelligence to be assessed.'

Being young and awestruck by film stars at that time, Telephonist Primrose Skinner 'felt quite honoured having Rex Harrison and Raymond Huntley stationed with us at Uxbridge. Mind you, we didn't feel too good, after being on night shift and looking like nothing on earth, to see Rex's handsome tanned face first thing in the morning, when he was going on duty.'

Newton was a Polish Flying Training Unit where Olive Houghton was stationed as a Parachute Packer. 'I well remember a young Polish airman coming to the Parachute Section and shaking my hand to thank me for saving his life. He had bailed out with the parachute I had packed. I had a brooch sent to me from the parachute firm.'
    Winifred Smith explains a parachute tradition:

When an airman used his 'chute, ten shillings was forwarded to the WAAF packer. It was to say 'Thank you. I got down safely.' So everyone thought how wealthy we were, until we said we got none of this money. It was used to provide us all with the odd dance. I wasn't flattered to be told by a cousin, a pilot, that he preferred to crash his plane rather than use a 'chute. I have the little silver wings awarded to Packers after eight successful live dropped parachutes. Our wings we wore above our left pocket, while on duty.

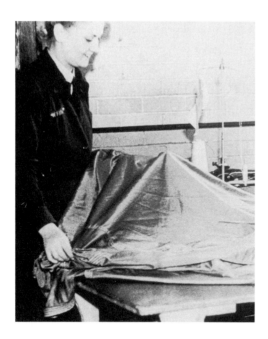

Parachute Packer at work, Ringway, 1944 (Winifred Smith)

In July 1941 the shortage of men at length overcame doubts as to whether airwomen had the strength to become Balloon Operators. It was a trade which they enjoyed, although it was abandoned before the war ended because the physical strain *did* prove too much for many women's constitutions. The only grouse voiced by Elizabeth Taverner was 'the sand! With the strong winds – and they came off the Atlantic at Port Talbot – we ate, drank and slept with sand. It found its way into everything.'

Airwomen often formed all-women crews, as was the case in this incident reported by Florence Dillon:

In the middle of one night the Duty Piquet woke me with, 'Sarge! We've lost the balloon.' A piece of shrapnel had hit it, and it was gradually deflating. In so doing it had managed to wind its cable around a council house chimney, and was nearby, bouncing up and down in the school yard.

Our plan was to get to it and pull the cord on it, which was designed to deflate it quickly. However, it tore the chimney off the house before we had time to winch it in.

The tenant of the house, meanwhile, had roused her husband with, 'Fred, wake up. The Germans are here!' (Our balloon crew must have sounded fearsome as we were racing through her garden.) It took me some time to explain to her what had really happened and where her chimney had gone.

A similar fate befell Irene Berkeley's crew. 'We left the balloon one night safely bedded down, but next morning it had vanished, only to be found in someone's garden, nose down, blocking the light out of the occupant's bedroom, and at the same time giving him the fright of his life!'

In a letter from Inverness, Doreen Strickland reported an incident in March 1941.

The other morning an Observer Corps man was patrolling when he saw a balloon trailing low over some fields. He grabbed the cable to prevent it from straying further, but naturally his weight was not enough to keep it down and he felt himself being trailed along in the wake of the balloon. To prevent it straying further, he obviously had to tie it to something steady, so round the middle of a cow was tied the cable, while the OC man made off to inform the authorities. No sooner was his back turned than there came a gust of wind and the poor bewildered cow sailed into the air. In the end, they had to cut the cow down and let the balloon go!

Balloon Operators bringing down the balloon, 1942
(Basil Beagent)

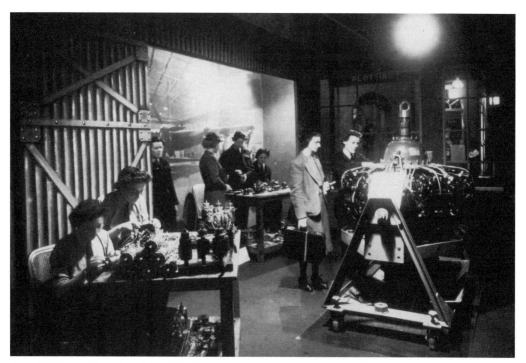

An exhibition at Harrods in July 1944, showing a comparison of WAAF trades between 1939 and 1944 (Edna Jarvis)

The trade of Tailoress was another later one to appear. Airwomen worked for the whole camp, mainly altering uniforms. There was, however, a slight hitch when Eileen James was asked at Harwell, 'to alter a dance dress for a WAAF Officer, as a favour. One of our girls accidentally burnt a hole in it as we worked. So we all got together and took a panel out. It was not even missed, and she looked much slimmer!' On another occasion a young Rear Gunner asked Eileen

if she would sew on the stripes for his promotion, put on his DFC (Distinguished Flying Cross) and sew his lucky charm under his Rear Gunner badge. Normally we would refuse, but he was going on leave next day and wanted to walk in on his parents and give them a surprise, so I said I would.

We would hear the planes going out and count them in, but this time there was one missing. I got this horrible feeling that it was him. I was right. He did not come back. I had to take his uniform to the Adjutant, and when I did I burst out crying. Often afterwards I wished he had left his lucky compass under the old battledress badge he always wore!

Airwomen were also employed as Meteorology Assistants. While working in the Met. Office, Jean Zaczek and others 'had to polish the Met. Office floor. So we made our smallest Forecaster stand on the mop as we pushed it, to get a good shine! We also loved saluting our Met. Officer Forecasters, when they were on bicycles! They were suddenly put into uniform in 1944 and had no Air Force training. They nearly fell off their bikes, trying to respond.'

By the end of the war airwomen were employed in nineteen purely WAAF trades and in seventy-four open to airmen and airwomen, without counting the twenty-three WAAF Officer branches. Indeed, there were very few trades in which they were *not* involved – mainly those requiring physical strength or combatant status.

9
TECHNICAL WORK

As early as 1937 Robert Watson–Watt was convinced that women would be ideal for operating Radar. They had the requisite 'alertness, keenness and delicacy of touch . . . could do three things at once . . . and were quick thinking and conscientious'. And so it proved! They were already manning Radar (then called RDF) in October 1939, and thousands of women kept their work secret!

'Our first night at Lizard Point, Cornwall, turned out to be extremely rough, with a gale blowing,' observes Betty Bonner.

Oboe, Radar Ground Station, Strathallan, 1944 (RSRE Malvern)

So the four girls going on watch were tied together like rock-climbers, and led along a narrow muddy cliff-edge by an RAF Regiment Sergeant with a torch to find our Operations Cabin – Susie – and we all finished up lost in the middle of a field!

Our wooden toilet, also in the middle of a field near the Operations Cabin, lost its door during one of the storms and this meant that two of the watch had to leave the Ops Cabin at a time, one to hold the door up!

Of this, our Mad Mech wrote the following poem:

> Misfortune is haunting the Ladies of Lizard,
> Who live in the land of perpetual blizzard.
> The Station's Defence just pretend to be blind,
> Since their WC door has now, 'Gone with the Wind'! .

'At one point, Technical COs were asked for suggestions for the destruction of our equipment in the event of invasion,' says Stella Cottman. 'Our very nervous Canadian, badly injured in Ventnor bombing, suggested a land-mine under our Radar Cabin, with the detonating button in his office. We were most relieved when his suggestion was turned down!'

Even in the best of conditions, things did not always go according to plan. On one occasion Stella, now a Corporal, was 'requested to check our calibration, since we appeared to have plotted one of the naval escorts overland. Later, we received a rare apology from the Navy, as an escort had in fact run aground off Stranraer!'

Pat Sparks remembers another story: 'Everyone was puzzled by blurs and smears on our Radar screen. Technicians were going frantic, as they could not trace the fault. Eventually someone discovered the LAC on duty at our aerial, two fields away, had been using his new electric razor, plugged into the terminal!'

One day two Australian aircrew came to see Jean Dingwall and her shift in the Bawdsey Radar Operations Room. 'They told us that we had patiently tracked and plotted their aircraft for hour after hour as it limped across the North Sea after a raid. It was very gratifying to know that we had played a part in saving their lives.'

'Without doubt, we had one of the most interesting and worthwhile jobs,' declares Joyce Smith, a Radar Operator at Kenley,

helping to save hundreds of ditched pilots from the hostile waters of the English Channel and the North Sea, as part of the team work of Air-Sea Rescue.

Without an accurate 'fix' on a pilot before he baled out, the searching aircraft would not have known where to locate him.

We received a generous tribute by letter after the big pick-up of 119 aircrew on 6–7 September 1943, 'for our efficiency in fixing, which played a prominent part in the success of the operation'. Kenley was involved in the rescue of 85 of those 119 aircrew.

Stella Buist goes on to recount the odd story of Winkie the pigeon (pigeons occasionally accompanied the crew of some Second World War planes).

One day in February 1942, one Beaufort out of a flight of six was missing after an operation over the North Sea. She was M for Mother, from our 42 Squadron. The search seemed hopeless. Then a ray of hope! A pigeon had returned to its loft at Broughton Ferry, dirty and oil-stained. Yes! It was one from M42. The Station Navigation Officer quickly worked out how far the pigeon had flown – 120 miles – which narrowed down the search area to about half. Our aircraft were given the new position and before long a Hudson pilot of the Royal Dutch Naval Air Service radioed that he had sighted a dinghy with survivors in it. Three stations took a bearing on the Hudson and a message was sent to a High Speed Launch of the Air-Rescue Service. After 20 hours at sea, all four crew of the Beaufort M42 were picked up safely by the launch. And it had all been made possible by the endurance of Winkie, the little carrier pigeon! It was later awarded the Dickin Medal for Animal Bravery!

In 1944 terrifying weapons were used against the civilian population in the form of the VIs and V2s. Many people, like Denise Wynn who was working at Bawdsey, knew beforehand.

We had to attend a special lecture, which was very secret! It was about V2s and how we could be using special equipment to try to pinpoint the mobile launching sites as the rockets were fired. We were also trained to develop films, which operated automatically when we pressed a button on sight of a V2 on our screens, which were set vertically.

I remember getting very tired on these machines. My eyelids would droop and I literally had to hold my eyelids up to stop falling asleep. Our concentration had to be intense as the rocket flashed through our range of view in fractions of a second.

A Radar Operator at Bawdsey, 1944 (Elaine Dew and *Illustrated London News*)

A well-kept secret, only recently revealed, was that the UK was saved from an even worse weapon late in the war, partly owing to the work of the Radar girls. According to Group Captain Cheshire, 'this was the V3 – a huge cannon hidden under 50 feet of reinforced concrete, which when ready would be able to pump a 200 lb bomb every 10–20 minutes into London'. Fortunately Bomber Command destroyed the pinpointed site of this 100-foot-long, Coender multi-barrelled pump gun and its rocket-assisted shells before it was completed.

Certain Radar Operators like Betty Bonner were eventually trained as Radar Mechanics.

I recall receiving an irate call from a pilot, complaining that our pylon navigation light was not on and that he had almost flown into it. I made a laborious climb to the top of the pylon – 360 feet – in the dark to change the bulb, to find the joke was on me! It was one of the RAF mechanics claiming to be a pilot. This was just after the war finished, of course.

Plotters were another 'secret' trade, recruited right at the beginning of the war and called Clerks SD (Special Duties). During the height of the Battle of Britain, Joyce Williams was manning a direct line to the Observer Corps at Truro,

who kept enquiring, in their own inimitable drawl, 'Are you there, St Eval?', or, 'Are you all right, St Eval?', for they could see the flames and fires caused by the incendiaries!

Later we moved to a stone-built barn, hastily converted for us into an Operations Room. In the early hours of one morning there was the crump crump of bombs, which hit the NAAFI and killed several people. The entrance to this Ops Room was via a midden where sheep were inclined to pay visits on several occasions – no doubt German spies in disguise!

In 1941 Phyllis Smart laments the closing of her old Operations Block.

> Goodbye old Ops, tis true we loved thee not,
> Those iron doors, whose verberating clang
> Echoed and re-echoed through the dim ways,
> Will ope no more. Shut fast they will remain,
> Until some far day.
> Goodbye to draughty nights and stifling days,
> When air came in, in gales or else it failed
> To come at all. Farewell to Stygian gloom,
> When lighting failed and we had fumy light
> Of incandescent.
> Goodbye to puffy eye and haggard cheek, [Ops Eye]

> To headache, earache and to listlessness,
> To creeping sloth and lack of 'joie de vivre', [Ops Complaint]
> And all those other ills to which our flesh
> Is heir unwilling.

The picture graphically displayed by Plotters in Operations Rooms enabled the RAF to send up only those aircraft needed to counter the invading flights, thus economizing in precious planes and petrol. It was the saving of the RAF and the country!

In order to remind Plotters like Alma Jones 'that the arrows and plaques we used on the maps represented precious live pilots and valuable Spitfires, we were taken to meet them at Northolt. One or two were in pressure tanks, where they unwound slowly from lack of oxygen (effects similar to deep-sea divers). We were then taken to see the special high-flying Spitfires!'

Another airwoman, Marguerite Riley,

> was on duty in the Ops Room, which was underground and not too far from the coast. One night we heard a terrible sound like bumping. When we investigated, we saw that it was a heavy shell, which had dug its nose into the ground above the place where we were working. It was then discovered that it was a torpedo, fired by a German U-boat. The fact that it had not exploded saved our lives! When we had pulled ourselves together, we began to joke about it. We said that we had been torpedoed on dry land!

Air-conditioning, which was meant to keep the air fresh in underground Operations Blocks, was sometimes switched off in case of gas attacks. On one such occasion, Mavis Pickford relates, 'the Group Captain rang down from the fishbowl above, during the night, to say that the combined smell of fish and chips, beer and scent was becoming overpowering. Could I ask the girls not to use 'Evening in Paris' quite so liberally on night duty?'

After their success as Plotters, airwomen were considered for more responsible posts. Doreen Strickland gives a lighthearted view of her work:

> Who does juggling tricks with telephones,
> Most wondrous to see?
> Who bobs up and down and writes and talks,
> Makes noise enough for three?

Scene in Biggin Hill Operations Room, 1944, by WAAF
artist Elva Blacker (Phyllis Chaundy)

Who keeps shouting to the ROC, the Ack Ack and DC?
Who? The Uncrowned Natter Queen of Ops,
That harassed type – Ops B!

When the sun shines you may think it's grand
To have a lovely day,
But poor Ops B, fine weather tends
To send her hair quite grey.
Every blessèd thing is airborne –
Ops B just finds time to say
In tone of resignation,
'*Sauve qui peut*', and, 'Come what may!'

When her switchboard leaps to sudden life,
And all the lights go red,
She answers Grangemouth and then finds
Balado Bridge instead!
She can't hear them, they can't hear her,

And a bawling contest starts;
'What?' 'Hello' 'Speak up, can't hear you', –
These are the politest parts!

Then a furious voice at Tealing says,
'Oh Turnhouse, is that you?
I've been on this line, *five* minutes ringing,
Ringing without getting through!'

PBX goes red, a voice says,
''Ello Miss, 'ere's 341,
Moments 22, 26 airborne,
Our air firing 'as begun.
Wot's the range in use this morning,
Air to air and air to sea?'
Ops B says, relief abounding,
'Ask the SGO, not me!'

'We've got a dozen Spitfires
Up at 30,000 feet,'
Says a distant voice from Grangemouth.
Ops B leaps up from her seat,
Says in tones of irritation,
'This makes everything complete!
Don't you know you should have told us?'
'Yes, I'm sorry!' says the voice
Ops B drops her phone and mutters
Epithets both strange and choice!

Then a muffled voice at Errol
Shouts, 'Hello Ops. Is that you?
Duty Pilot here, reporting
One aircraft that's overdue.
It's a Mustang and was coming
All the way from Chipping Norton.'
'That's OK,' says Ops B. 'It has
Only just pancaked at Scorton!'

Louder yet the noise increases,
Through it all Controller sits,
Coping with a hundred aircraft,
Typhoons, Beaus, Daffys and Spits! . . . [Beauforts, Defiants,
                                                    Spitfires]

So with Signals, Forms and Escorts,
Prangs and Panics, goes the day.
Just sometimes a Hun comes calling,
But he doesn't often stay
Long enough, but hell for leather
Streaks home, speeded on his way
By the Typhoons and the Spitfires
From the Forth, the Tweed and Tay.

But an end must come to all things –
Even for the poor Ops B
Comes relief, and off she totters,
Homeward bound for lunch or tea.
Softly, as she leaves Kinellan,
Whispers, 'Oh well, RIP!
Any cans left to be carried,
Won't be carried now by me.'

The work of Kathleen Fox was also top secret: 'Watchkeepers knew every detail of an operation over enemy territory before even the Station Commander. The watchkeeper was responsible for keeping an eye and an ear on every detail of what was happening and seeing to it that the right person or people were fully informed. We *never* discussed our work outside the Operations Room. Our lips were sealed!'

By 1941, despite a great shortage of manpower, the RAF still did not believe airwomen would be able to manage the technical trades. This was really not surprising, given the almost total lack of opportunities for girls to study sciences in most schools, regardless of their excellent general education. Nevertheless, spurred on by necessity, a few skilled trades were broken down into simpler elements. Thus the Instrument Mechanics, Charging Board Operators and Sparking Plug Testers emerged.

NCOs of D Watch Plotters at Barton Hall, 1943 (Joyce Williams)

Airmen took to these strange newcomers very well, if somewhat roughly! As a Sparking Plug Tester, Emily Riley

must have said something to some airmen in our hangar, and the next thing I knew they had picked me up and put me in the petrol bath we used for washing our sparking plugs. Luckily I was in a thick boiler suit!

Another day, some of us had gone for our break at the Church Army Hut and there was loads of snow around. Of course I couldn't resist snowballing the men, but I came off worst. Some of the airmen rolled me in the snow back to the hangar where I worked. I must have looked like a snowman!

By 1943 these trades had disappeared, since by then it had been discovered that, after training, selected airwomen in the so-called 'experimental' trades were quite capable of more difficult work. Airwomen were thus introduced to the

Testing R/T Equipment in the cockpit of a Blenheim, 1943 (Daisy Hills)

technical trades, first as Mechanics and later, but in smaller numbers, at the even more exacting level of Fitter!

A different type of trade was Radio Telephone (R/T) Operator, which made its appearance in 1941. Girls had to have clear speaking voices, as they worked in Flying Control and spoke direct to the pilots. 'R/T watch was kept for all 24 hours,' points out Daphne Richardson.

This was mainly for Mayday calls [from the French *m'aidez* – help me], which meant that an aircraft was in trouble or lost. When I was at Gosport, most of the calls came from American pilots, whose navigation was not too hot! They couldn't understand why they were on the south coast, when they should have been in Scotland!

I also put up my greatest black there. I gave permission for an aircraft to land, when the pilot asked me to put out a pail of water. But to my dismay, when I looked out of the Control Office, I saw an old Walrus flying boat coming low over the runway. Fortunately he didn't land, but it took me a long time to live it down!

In 1940 – before the R/T Operators – WAAF Wireless Operators appeared. Among them were the Special Operators of the Y Listening Service, where, Jean Kightley explains, 'highly secret work was performed, in the main, by German-speaking refugees from Europe – many Jewish – who, in exposed positions on the south coast, logged and passed to Bletchley Park [Station X] all the German transmissions that they could pick up.' One such was Barbara Hughes: 'Took up position in Wireless Operators' room on usual set. Received and intercepted messages from German aircraft mostly in code, and ground station replies. Cheadle where I worked, was supposed to be a secret station, although we knew the Germans knew about us.'

At Hornchurch Joy Selwood found it necessary 'to pass through a field of cows to man our Listening Post. One night I found the cows wandering down the lane. I returned and told the farmer. His only reply was to lean out of the window, hand me a stick and tell me to get them back into the field.'

At Chicksands Priory, working for Y Service and using the Enigma machine to break German codes in the messages thus monitored and recorded, Joyce Meeks and others there were early subjects of industrial psychology:

We were actually given four days and nights more leave than was given to other airwomen; because of our very hard work, strain and none of the fun as at other stations. We spent these extra four days at a mansion called Clifton House. We were permitted to wear civvies and had morning tea brought to us in our bedrooms. There were four airwomen to a room – a blue room, a green room, a yellow room and so on – and we were *served* with meals at the table!

'Gone for a Burton', a familiar term today, had its origins in the RAF as Irene Bell and several others attest. 'It usually referred to the loss on Operations of an aircraft and its crew. But it appears that this originated in Blackpool, when we would-be Wireless Operators took our final exams in a room over the shop of Burton, the Tailor!'

In 1942 at Cranage Elizabeth André

was involved in a training programme for aircraft. We all had to communicate with one another in Q Code. At one moment I received an unusual signal. I looked it up and found it meant, 'Tail on fire. What must I do?' Telephoning the Control Tower, I gave them the message. The Officer shouted, 'Bale out, you fool!' Without bothering about Q Code, I sent in plain language exactly what the Officer said. The crew landed safely and we were all relieved!

Two airwomen working on a Mobile Direction Finding Van, which gave bearings to incoming aircraft in order to help the Control Tower (Gwyneth Pritchard)

In mid-1944, at Hooton, Ellen Duckworth had

a Station Commander, who believed that we should experience the problems of operating the wireless in the air. I was asked if I was prepared to fly. After several trips, not very successful as my log-book went, another WAAF Wireless Operator, Corporal Instructor, pilot and myself, took off in an Avro Anson. I operated on the return leg and actually got it right, received permission to land, completed my log-book and sat back, when there was a great thump and I found myself standing in a few inches of muddy water. The plane was sitting in the middle of the Mersey on a sandbank! . . .

The Medical Officer and the stretcher party appeared on the horizon and I was urged off the wing, where I now was, into the mud. My WAAF friend disappeared with one party and I ended up in a dinghy without oars. My log-book was used instead to propel us across the deeper channels until we reached the sea wall. I don't know how I climbed it, but I did, because I remember later passing my parachute down to a dear old man in a rowing boat, who grabbed it by its D handle and it billowed open. So clutching yards of nylon we were rowed across the Eastham Canal, which runs along the airfield. My poor log-book! It was unreadable and no one ever knew how good I had been!

Wireless Mechanics – a more skilled trade – were a later arrival during the war. When Blanche Gage was sent to a different section on her station, even the airmen found her a bit of a surprise:

Eventually I arrived at a group of huts and aircraft. I propped my bike outside and walked in.

There was a deathly silence. I have never seen such a scruffy group of airmen in my life! All needed a shave, their collars were filthy and their hats . . .! I said, 'I'm the Radio Mechanic. Who's in charge?' One of them silently pointed to an office marked WO. As I went in, he put the phone down. At least *he* was clean and tidy! He said, 'We aren't used to women out here, but you won't have any trouble. The aircrew do the Daily Inspections. You put right any snags they report. Most of it will be finger trouble. OK?'

Back in the workshop every man was bent diligently over his bench. When

Two Wireless Mechanics who have finished work on an Airspeed Oxford aircraft at Little Rissington, 1944 (Vera Higginson)

Flight Mechanic and her aircraft. Spitalgate, 1945 (Phyllis Moore)

I went to get my tools from my bike, I saw someone had chalked on the door, 'Ssh – WAAF inside!'

A busload of aircrew arrived. The Wireless Operators' AGs collected an accumulator each and departed to their aircraft. When later one came back to say, the 'Press to speak' didn't work, I was pointed out to him as the Mechanic. The look of utter disbelief on his face was a picture. 'Can you fix it?' he asked. I didn't answer but unobtrusively crossed my fingers. Fortunately it was just a loose connection.

By midday word was around, 'The Wireless Mechanic is a WAAF!' and an amazing number of pilots and navigators had apparently to come in to speak to the Corporal about something and look over this strange object with wireless equipment. The Warrant Officer said, 'You'd better take one-and-a-half hours for lunch. It's quite a ride!' In the Mess I met my friends and told them how glad I was all the faults reported were trivial (although at the end of the week I found myself rewiring a main panel with thirty-two connections and 'Thank God it all worked,' when I had finished).

I cycled back to C Flight after lunch, and when I walked in, what a transformation! Every man had shaved and put on a clean collar. The floor had been swept and it was tidy. Just then the Sergeant arrived and stopped dead. 'Good God! Is it payday?' Nobody answered, but all pretended to be very busy. The Sergeant said, 'If they do this for a married WAAF, just think what they'd do for a single one!'

That afternoon was just like the morning. Sometimes I suspected that snags were reported, just to see if 'that WAAF' could fix them. The Australians were particularly sceptical of women Mechanics.

I was out on C Flight for a week. The Warrant Officer said he was sorry I was going, but on the other hand he thought the strain of being always polite and watching their language was more than many of the airmen could manage for a longer period!

When they first appeared Flight Mechanics were not taken seriously, but were treated kindly by the airmen. Mr Bentley, a Corporal Aero-Engine Fitter, was delighted

when the lady technical types arrived and we found many of them very helpful in the intricate jobs to be undertaken on aircraft engines. When changing the sparking plugs on the Rolls Royce Merlin engines, a spark plug would occasionally fall out of the end of the spanner and disappear down the V of the cylinder blocks. This entailed probing about with a wire and magnets for a considerable time. Then one day, one of the WAAF discovered that she could get her arm down between the cylinder blocks and the manifold, and retrieve the plug. Maria, as she was known, was then in great demand throughout the Squadron!

'While I was on my Flight Mechanics' course on engines, we were taught the names of different tools. I recall thinking that the instructor was swearing when he talked of a "Bastard" File,' admits Lily Yates. 'My father had a good laugh when I told him later.'

In the same context Alice Neighbour points out, 'as a WAAF Flight Mechanic, we were a new breed and personally I was amazed at the size of a Wellington bomber. I encountered the usual "Golden Rivet" ruse (supposedly the last rivet on the aircraft), and being sent for "sky hooks", with which the airmen tried to catch us out!'

Nancy Mowbray faced another kind of trial in her first weeks:

I was on Duty Crew the day a Lancaster took off, and I was one of the Duty Crew detailed to stand by to take the chocks away.

Although I did that job every day on the Wellingtons and thought nothing of it, I was not prepared for the slip-stream from a Lancaster. My navy beret was blown away and it took all my courage not to follow it. The dreadful feeling that I would be sucked into the propellers added to my fear!

The work of bringing in an aircraft also had its attendant dangers, giving Lily Grubb the fright of her life and nearly killing her.

It entailed us running backwards for about a mile. It was the third York aircraft at Riccarton Common which I had brought in that night under an hour. The pilot thought I was an airman and instead of accepting my hand signals to proceed slowly, he revved up. I couldn't keep up with his pace and being only about six feet ahead of him, I had to throw myself down into the greasy ditch and let him proceed. He nearly took off the roof of the Duty Crew Hut. Later he was most apologetic, but my Sergeant told me to bring in the very next aircraft to prevent any nerves overtaking me. That was the worst moment of my career!

There was also the danger, experienced more than once by WAAF like

Margaret Houghton at Hibaldstow – her Spitfire was nicknamed T for Trouble – of taking off on the tail of the plane on which they were working. And there could be other unpleasant accompaniments as described graphically by George Carter, an Aero-Engine Fitter:

> As was usual with most fighter planes, unless the tail was weighed down while the engine revved up to its full power, the plane would nose over. However, the risk of becoming airborne was not the only discomfort or disaster, as when leaning or lying over the tail-plane, your backside was left exposed to the full force of the slip-stream and whatever may get caught in it. Thus the 'gentle rain from heaven' assumed monsoon-force proportions, as the mighty Rolls Royce engine reached full throttle. A split second and the seat of your overalls, plus all that was within, would have reached saturation point. Should the rain turn to hail, then your buttocks received a lashing comparable to that administered by the proverbial public school birch-rod. There was also the occasional pebble, whipped up, and with missile-like propulsion and precision, precipitated into the dead centre of your posterior, bringing a wish that the RAF had stuck with hot-air balloons! It was a real BUM duty to get lumbered with. It was also the point at which the chance of flying off into the 'wild blue yonder', became a real possibility!

In 1944 Emily Little wrote the following verses about her work:

> The Lords of the Air they call us,
> They speak of our growing fame,
> The front page of each newspaper
> Is adorned with the pilot's name.
> In stories of deeds and valour,
> Written up into the sky,
> You read of high speed battles
> Fought by the men who fly!
>
> But there's one who gets no medals,
> You will never hear her name,
> She does not fly in the pale blue sky
> Nor pose for the news with a plane.
> Her job can't be called romantic,

My ACW2 (John Barnes)

Nor for the public gaze,
But the Lords of the Air respect her,
And often give her praise!

Who inspects the kite [plane] each morning?
Who fills up the tanks each night?
Who keeps the engine always sweet?
And keeps all the pressures right?
Who is up at the crack of dawning?
And still there when the twilight fades?
Pulling her weight of keeping the crate
Ready to fly on raids!

So next time you see a picture
Of a plane and its smiling crew,
Remember the lass who keeps it aloft,
Is an ACW2!

And next time you praise the pilot
As the enemy faces wreck,
Remember the girl who does not fly:
The Humble and Proud Flight Mech.

Kathleen Moore records a heartwarming incident in her career as a Flight Mechanic Electrician:

During a dreadful winter, I was stationed at Little Rissington. Life was very hard. Snow blizzards continued and eventually the camp was cut off and food supplies were running short. The men had to dig the road out which connected us to the village of Bourton-on-the-Water. There had been no flying for weeks and all the Flights were congregated together in the hangar.

One day as Jock and I were about to leave, Chiefy [Chief Technician] came in and asked if we would go and unblock a pitot-head, which had frozen up. He pointed out directions where we would find the plane and we set off.

We trudged on and on. The snow was thick and hard. I hadn't noticed that the normally happy, talkative Jock was unusually quiet. In my mind, I was questioning what on earth I was doing, out in this God-forsaken white wilderness. Siberia couldn't possibly be worse. For the first time after nearly four years in the WAAF I felt homesick. I imagined just coming in the door at home, to see and feel the warmth of a big fire roaring up the chimney, and the smell of hot buttered toast coming from the kitchen.

Perhaps I sniffed out loud, or perhaps it was just a sigh? Jock suddenly turned to me and said, 'Oh Kiddo. This is bloody hell for me, but what it must be like for you, I can't imagine.' He put a comforting arm around my shoulder and we trudged on.

Suddenly on the horizon we spotted an object. It was like seeing an oasis in the desert, only the reverse, and I wondered which was the worse, the searing heat or this terrible cold. In unison we both cried 'the Kite'!

We reached it at last, its wheels almost buried in deep snow. We scraped away at the carpet of snow from the canopy over the cockpit and with some persuasion managed to prise open the door. Jock bravely volunteered to free the offending pitot-head, while I sat inside and watched the air speed indicator. It was some time before the needle swung over, indicating it was clear and the wind flowing through. Poor Jock clambered into the co-pilot's seat, blowing and rubbing his frozen hands.

For a brief time we sat and queried the wisdom of the Powers that Be. It would be impossible for this plane to take off or even be moved across the frozen ground. So why had they wanted this job done? With the mysteries of the Powers that Be remaining unresolved, and the darkening sky a harbinger of the gathering snowstorm, we set off to face the two mile or so trek, back across the frozen snow to the warmth of the hangar.

To be a WAAF Fitter was indeed to be one of a rare breed. As a member of this élite group, Doreen Gaskin found that

the first time we girls – Airframes, Engines and Electricians – had to work on a plane by ourselves to prove we were capable, the pilots refused to take it up!

Flight Lieutenant May was ordered to do this, and he refused unless *all* the women went too. It was hilarious! We girls were so terrified, never having been on a plane before, let alone repair it!

We had parachutes and I was with two other girls in the cockpit. The others were in various parts of the plane and, on take off, the escape hatch over the pilot's head blew open. The girl beside me, an Electrician who hadn't learned how a plane flies, was so scared that she pulled the rip-cord of her parachute, and the cockpit was swamped. This marvellous pilot then flew the plane a couple of circuits and returned to base. The whole station was watching. The pilot gave us a wonderful report on our good work and after that we were one of the boys!

Irene Fairlie became a Corporal Fitter on Airframes. She vividly remembers one incident, when she and her crew were checking the personal plane of

the Air Commodore in Charge of 17 Group Coastal Command, based at Turnhouse, Edinburgh. He was a fearsome Officer and all quailed before him. He meant to take off at short notice. Refuelling was being done by a Lancashire lad, an Engine Mechanic, to moans of 'Get a move on, airman!' Several of us were around, chocks ready for off, when the erk, Johnny, put his foot through the mainplane. There was a crashing of splinters, a hole two feet square and many oaths! The outrage was beyond words, with the AOC apoplectic. All the servicing crew collapsed, hysterical with mirth, notwithstanding the august presence. It is still one of the funniest things I ever saw.

In addition to these many and varied WAAF trades, there were some airwomen who volunteered for other work, which involved them in temporarily leaving the WAAF. These were also among the most dangerous, as well as skilful, duties which called for the greatest courage. Thus among the girls who worked for the Special Operations Executive (SOE) were fifteen who went on Active Service with the Resistance in German-occupied France (see my book *Mission Improbable*).

'As I was posted to Kemble in Transport Command, work varied,' says Hilda Bell.

At Kemble we received the planes straight from the factories flown by pilots of the Air Transport Auxiliary, some quite famous – Jim Mollinson for one. When the plane arrived we had to find out where they were destined, as at that time most were being sent to North Africa. So we adjusted the plane to make it able to fly in the conditions of the Middle East.'

There were some airwomen who had been allowed to volunteer for the ATA, who actually flew these planes! Sometimes they even caused surprise among the WAAF. As a new four-engined Stirling bomber was being delivered to her station

Three WAAF of the Air Transport Auxiliary, 1945. The girl on the left is from Ceylon (Frankie Horsburgh)

from the factory, Phyllis Cove, an MT Driver, 'was detailed to pick up the ferry pilot and go to the Officers' Mess, where food and transport was laid on. I waited near the pan, when the bomber taxied in. After a few moments, the door to the aircraft opened and out stepped a slim, petite blonde. I had expected a strapping man!'

On evening shift one summer Joyce Killip, a Meteorologist, was present 'when one of our intrepid women ferry pilots called Flying Control for permission to land the fighter plane she was delivering, as she was off course and had been airborne longer than usual. They thought it might be a refuelling job, but she came rushing into our Met. Office on the ground floor, saying, "Where is it?" After being shown the WAAF toilet, she dashed back to her plane and took off, somewhat pink-faced, but with many thanks.'

AC2 Billy Brown

> In these bustling, back-slapping, gong-award days
> The WAAF have not had their full meed of praise:
> So just give a thought to the jobs which they do
> And all raise your caps to our partners in blue.
>
> Metwomen, batwomen, clerks and wops,
> Cooks and plotters and tele ops,
> Flight mecs, stewards and DMTs
> Equipment assistants and orderlies.
>
> MT mechanics and RDF ops,
> Instrument bashers and Service cops,
> Balloon operators and just plain GDs
> (And to others I've missed, my apologies.)

10
FACING DANGER TOGETHER

For airwomen who worked on airfields, death was never far away. While standing in a queue for the camp bus to Loughborough, Sybil Stansfield saw 'three of our bombers crash on landing over the airfield, one after another. We knew all the crews and in fact, some of us had made dates with them.'

Airwomen wept into their pillows at night but carried on, always hoping that disaster would not hit 'their' boys. In the summer of 1942 at Honington, Betty Thomson

had come off duty on Operations during the night's raid on Germany, where

Helping to adjust a Canadian pilot's helmet of 72 Hurricane Squadron at Acklington, May 1941. He died later, shot down over the Channel (Marjory Ross)

I knew that the aircraft – Wellingtons – were carrying a big load of incendiaries. As darkness fell we heard the aircraft take off. Suddenly the familiar noises sounded wrong. Then there was an almighty crash and something had come down. Smoke and flames rose from a field about three-quarters of a mile away.

The new RAF doctor rushed for his car, although he was off duty and didn't know his way around in the dark yet, so I went with him. We drove as fast as possible to the edge of the field, scrambled through the hedge and were immediately transfixed by the sight of a Wellington enveloped in smoke and flames. The heat was too great to get anywhere near. Incendiaries were exploding and the glare lit up the sky. The rescue services stood helplessly by and we watched appalled by the sight!

Suddenly, out from the ditch, crawled five smoke-blackened figures. 'They're out!', the shout went up. It was quite a moment!

Airwomen worked in many different places, scattered over a large airfield and were often involved in the danger themselves, as Valerie Pearman-Smith recounts:

Early in the Bombing Offensive at Waterbeach, when Stirlings were still front-line aircraft, one of the Section Officers, WAAF G, was Jo Easton. Towards the end of take-off for Operations, Jo was cycling along the perimeter track on her way to see her airwomen in their various places of work, when a Stirling crashed on take-off and caught fire immediately. Jo flung her bicycle down at the side of the perimeter and ran to the blazing aircraft. She went in and started to drag out crew members. I think she got at least one of them out, but then the bomb load exploded, killing her and the remaining crew on the aircraft.

We all took the view that it had been a great act of bravery on the part of a very young Section Officer, and we expected she would be awarded a posthumous George Cross. But the Powers that Be took the view that Jo shouldn't have been on the airfield at night. Being on the airfield constituted not leaving the peri-track. Jo was awarded a posthumous Mention in Dispatches!

Indeed, when you worked on an airfield it was never wise to relax your concentration, even for a moment, as Sheila Jollie discovered at Bruntingthorpe:

By 2200 hours the remaining aircraft have returned and landed safely, so night flying is over and so is my shift. I leave the Control Tower to cycle back along the perimeter track. It is dark and cloudy. Then suddenly a roar of engines and a huge black shape looms over my head, with about two feet or less of clearance. I just keep cycling – and the aircraft flies straight on, the wheel missing me by inches.

The pilot never knew! What I only found out later was that an aircraft from our Satellite Airfield had returned late and was ordered to land here. I was very badly shaken by my brush with death, and no one, officially, knew what had happened!

While working at Leuchars, Stella Buist had the thrill many times of knowing that her station had been able to save an aircraft. Even though for her part she was only a humble Clerk she felt as much involved as any.

The airfield had been quite suddenly enveloped in thick fog and a matronly Oxford, on practice, was still airborne. We switched on the Lorenz Beam [used for blind approach training] though we did not think the Oxford would be able to land even with that aid; we could not see the perimeter track outside our windows! The flare party was sent out, but before the flares could be lit the Oxford had landed. The Pilot told us later that he had touched down slightly to one side of the runway. It was marvellous to think the Beam had really worked. Now that we had proved its worth in a real emergency, we looked upon it with something akin to reverence.

The girls were always aware of their close proximity to war and its dangers. Joyce Collin-Smith gives an account of an operation at Lindholme, No. 1 Group, Bomber Command, in September 1942:

As we go over to the NAAFI for breakfast, we think, because of the mist, we probably shan't be operating tonight. The Tannoy blares out suddenly, 'Cider. It's Cider.' It means we may be operational after all! Groans all round. We've had a lot of losses recently and the Wellingtons are looking a bit battered.

Sergeant Boyd gallops in late and cross. Someone stuck over her bed recently, 'Here lies de Boyd what never catches de Woym'. She was not amused, but could not pin down the culprit!

At Station Headquarters I go up to Intelligence. We are upstairs and can look across the airfield to the wide flat landscape, up towards Doncaster. I'm making coffee for Squadron Leader Castle when the Tannoy announces, 'Brandy. It's Brandy.' That means we are definitely to be prepared for a bomber operation this night. Castle announces, 'It's Essen. And three Fresher Crews for Brest.'

[The crews are briefed.] As the Poles go out, Janek winks at me, Kostek smiles, Kazimierz walks stoopingly, Leo sneezes with a heavy cold, and Balbo, which means 'Beardy' because he was bearded during their long escape trek through the Carpathians two years ago, looks longingly at Sheila Catling and she at him.

At take-off time we are down in the Operations Room, steel walls and doors enclosing us. We have written up the huge wall blackboard . . . when you watch the bombing-up of aircraft, out there against the evening sky, black and menacing as the ground crews load them, you always know that one or two of the dispersal points will be empty in the morning. The hours of waiting are long, especially when you've got someone special up there!

As they come droning in, and the Control Tower comes through on the phone, we fill the board with the appropriate details. Squadron Leader Castle sends for me to go up to the Interrogation Room and help out as they are

A WAAF and Polish Officers of 308 Fighter Squadron from Lwow outside Exeter Cathedral after the ceremony of laying up their colours for safe-keeping, following their presentation to the city (Eileen Harding-Newman)

short-handed. The crew of S for Sugar troops in, some still in their sheepskins – all looking heavy-eyed and exhausted. We give them tea and smokes, but they are too tired to be interested. They've had a bad trip and they nearly always resent the long drawn out questioning, though they know it's essential.

They go off to bed and other crews come in. One has blood on his sleeve and news of some damage. Another has a dead man aboard. In the early hours I go down again to Operations and find Sheila Catling filling in the board with a drained face and stoical look. D for Donald is not back. Balbo . . .! 'They might have diverted to another airfield,' we say hopefully. But by first light we know there is no hope.

Janek is waiting outside, and comes from the shadows to say, 'I'll walk you to your quarters.'

They are deathly cold. There is no heating, never any hot water. We are used to it. Sheila is sitting on her bed shivering before the dying embers of the little fire. I stir it up and heat some milk to make cocoa for us both. She doesn't cry. Just cradles the mug in her hands, sipping and saying nothing.

In bed I hear her weep a little, quietly, beneath the blankets. He had been so courageous, so lively, so full of vigour and laughter, her dear Beardy. Outside the

Station Intelligence Section at work,
80 Wing, Radlett, 1945 (Joan Pearce)

fog draws in, heavy and thick. Tomorrow, surely, it will be time for a day of rest!

Catfoss was frequently used by Lancaster bombers, which had been damaged in a raid and could not make it back to home base. As a Wireless Operator, Ann Sinclair noted, 'there were sad occasions when the aircraft crashed on landing and the crew didn't survive, but at other times, in the early hours of the morning, Ops door would open and in would come men who were grimed and streaked with sweat and dirt, looking immeasurably tired and bearing no relationship to the bomber crews you see in films.'

Joan Schneider recounts in her diary another operation in which she was affected:

Back after lunch. Operations tonight. Wonder if my brother will be on the raid. That is when I get a tight feeling in my stomach that lasts until it is over.

At tea, I find my brother will be on the coming raid. I try to eat but something is bothering me. Must take a walk. I leave the base, walk a mile-and-a-half, and sit by a small river where time stands still. I look at the trees, listen to the birds and wonder what dreadful evil has brought this to our beautiful land. In the distance I can hear the engines of our Lancasters. I think of all the brave boys who fly them, wanting to reach out to them and bring them back.

In bed I can't sleep. Awake for hours. Then the sound of engines. One's stomach starts to unfold with a mixture of fear and for what the day will hold. All I can think of is my brother!

On duty, I have permission to call my brother's base – Pocklington. I ask for him. After what seemed a lifetime, the girl says she will put me through to the Adjutant. I know then he has gone. I go to church to pray hard for all the boys.

I was in church on the Sunday morning four months later, when a WAAF ran in to tell me that my brother was safe and a Prisoner of War. The little church on the base meant everything to us all!

When inexplicable things went wrong on his flight, the pilot usually blamed it on Gremlins – a peculiar, mischievous, Air Force species of sprites. This poem about them was sent by Stella Buist:

> When you're seven miles up in the heavens
> (That's a hell of a lonely spot!)
> And it's fifty degrees below zero,
> Which isn't exactly hot;

When you're frozen blue like your Spitfire,
And you're scared a Mosquito pink;
When you're thousands of miles from nowhere,
And there's nothing below but the drink,
It's then you will see the Gremlins,
Green and gamboge and gold,
Male and female and neuter,
Gremlins both young and old.
It's no good trying to dodge them –
The lessons you learned in the Link
Won't help you evade a Gremlin,
Though you boost and you dive and you jink.
White ones will wiggle your wing-tips,
Male ones will muddle your maps,
Green ones will guzzle your Glycol,
Females will flutter your flaps,
Pink ones will perch on your perspex,
And dance pirouettes on your prop.
There's a spherical middle-aged Gremlin
Who'll spin your stick like a top.
They'll freeze up your camera shutters,
They'll bite through your aileron wires,
They'll bend and they'll break and they'll batter,
They'll insert toasting forks in your tyres.
That is the tale of the Gremlins,
Told by the PRU –   [Photographic Reconnaissance Unit]
Pretty ruddy unlikely to many –
But fact, none the less, to The Few!

Even a long way from an airfield, accidents could occur. Hack Green was an Operational GCI Radar Station, where Florrie Phillips worked.

On 10 December 1943 a blanket of fog covered the whole area, and for some unknown reason my particular friend and I decided to get into the first transport to take us to our digs, and known as the 'old coach', instead of waiting for the rest of the crew who were travelling in the 'horse box'.

This day, sitting in the back seat of the 'old coach', as we crossed the

Transport taking Wireless Operators on duty at Chicksands, 1945 (Gwendoline Scase)

railway lines at the gated railway crossing, I suddenly saw the lamp of a railway engine almost on the gates of the crossing. I managed to keep quiet, realizing our driver might panic if I shouted, but as soon as we were safely over, there was an almighty bang and we stopped, to find that the train had crashed into the 'horse box' and carried its occupants some yards up the line. The scene was like a battlefield, with two dead and fourteen injured.

We did what we could for the injured, until Frank Furber, a local farmer, set up a first-aid post at his farm. Eventually the ambulances came from Crewe and the injured were taken to hospital in Wilmslow. A memorial service was held on the following Sunday in Nantwich Church, led by the Reverend Taylor Whittle.

On another occasion Elizabeth Lowder formed a very close friendship, while at Folly, with a girl called Miriam.

Not long after, I was posted to Branscombe and she had been sent to

Kidbrooke to do a Radar Mechanics course.

I was on duty on a certain night in February, when I came across a phenomenon – a newspaper! I was reading it when, to my horror, I saw the face of Miriam smiling up at me. She had been murdered! The shock of the discovery never left me. Later I learned that the man who had killed my friend was executed on, of all remarkable days, 6 June 1944!

Air raids were a frequent and often frightening occurrence, both on and off stations. The measures taken to combat them sometimes made them seem worse. Nottingham suffered its first air raid when Mary Slate was at Watnall: 'Clad in pyjamas, greatcoats and steel helmets, we all took shelter under our own beds. That night, the vibration from the local ack-ack guns was so intense that our beds jumped about the hut, closely followed by WAAF on all fours, chasing them!'

In 1942 at Netheravon a stray Dornier flew over Doreen Burd's camp 'in the early hours of the morning, firing its machine-guns. It did considerable damage to the WAAF Quarters – tearing up floors, walls, dislodging slates and even embedding a bullet in the bed-head of a WAAF Cypher Officer and showering her with pillow feathers! But no one was hurt. We presented an odd picture,

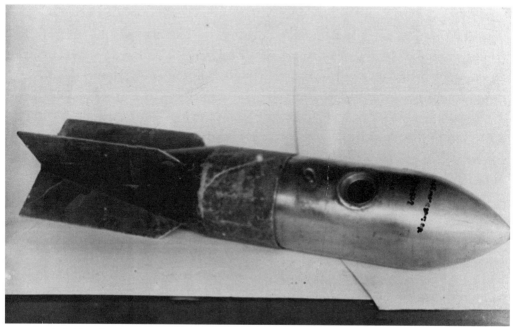

An unexploded bomb which was dropped near 257 Dispersal Hangar at Coltishall, 1942 (Dorothy Rixon)

jumping from our beds, many with curlers under their tin hats!'

In her diary for July 1942, Joyce Barrett at Torquay notes a strangely unsettling experience:

Lodged in a hotel that had been commandeered by the RAF. Met by a bowl of roses on the dressing table, filched by Geordie. Very touched by the sight of roses after three months of barracks! Hear a plane close by. Rush to the window. See a German plane level with me and a stick of bombs falling out. The young pilot stares across at me for a split second! I run to the basement shelter, shouting for others to follow. Just in time, as bombs explode!

The tip-and-run raider makes off over the sea, but it is immediately shot down by gunners on the cliffs. At the end of the day, I see that the tide has deposited the broken plane high on the beach, now guarded by the RAF Police. The pilot is dead, I am told.

In all the mayhem the girls could still be practical, despite their danger. One lunch-time, in the Equipment Section where Nora Tetsull worked, 'a WAAF took a mirror from stock and propped it up on the wall to make up her face. From nowhere came flying bullets. One passed by her ear and passed through the wooden structure. "Oo! Good thing it didn't break the mirror. That would have been seven years bad luck," was her only comment.'

In another such incident at Cottesmore, Joyce Stevenson remarked that 'no one was injured, but one girl was in tears because her stockings were ruined and would she have to pay for them?'

The surface Rest Hut at Joyce Dann's station 'was machine-gunned by enemy intruder aircraft, following our night fighters to our airfield when they were returning from patrol. Luckily the airwomen there were sleeping on the floor and the bullets were too high. I was blown through the Ops Entrance and hit its steel door, but I wasn't hurt much and could carry on with my R/T duties.'

Girls reacted to danger in different ways. When a lone raider zoomed over Odiham, Amy Southey, working as a Dental Hygienist, continued unmoved, despite the rat-tatting of bullets outside, which she fully expected to hit her. The Dental Officer, who was in the middle of drilling a tooth, also went on with his work. 'Then, out of the corner of my eye, I saw a movement. It was a small mouse! Instinctively, I gave one mighty yell and pulled up my legs on to the chair where I sat. I won't repeat what the Dental Officer said!'

The actual work of many airwomen often placed them directly in the firing line.

At her Dover Radar site, Elizabeth Kear frequently encountered heavy shelling from France. On the night of 29 January 1944 she and a friend, Mary, decided to try to get some sleep in the 'WAAF Only' shelter, as there were bunks in it.

Very crowded. Shared a lower bunk with Mary.

Suddenly the roof crashed down and the bunks collapsed. Total darkness, shouting, screaming and moaning. Found my torch in my greatcoat pocket and a few other torches appeared. End wall, steps and doorway had collapsed, and other end buried in debris. Realized we were buried. Awful silence apart from moaning. Mary had a head injury, with blood streaming down her face. As we were sleeping top to toe, it was my legs that were bleeding, but I was not hurt. Jean and Valerie in the bunk above were in a bad way. Jean had a part of her skull missing and Valerie was unable to move. No response from Daphne on the other side. Could not reach all of her.

Some time later – it seemed a lifetime – there were sounds from above and a face appeared from a hole in a pile of earth. The RAF had dug us out! Some girls were taken to hospital, the rest of us returned to our hut. My greatcoat and battledress were in tatters, but I only had minor cuts and bruises. I sat up in bed for the rest of the night unable to sleep. I was sent home on a three-day

An MT Ambulance Driver of a Balloon Squadron who was awarded a BEM for exceptional courage during the shelling of Dover, September 1944 (Kathleen Harding)

pass when I collapsed at work on Monday, still unable to sleep.

In memory of Jean Ramsey and Daphne Lewis who died, and many others who were seriously injured, please remember the 'Swingate Girls'!

Such disasters never came singly. Many miles away, in June 1944, while on a Wireless Operator and Morse Slip Reading Course, Gwendoline Scase witnessed 'the last ordinary bombing of London. A flying bomb made a direct hit on a block of billets, Thurloe Court. In our class of 24, only 6 escaped, of whom I was one. Of the 200 or so other students, 8 were killed and 60–70 injured.'

Perhaps the most fearsome devices deployed indiscriminately against the British population were the V1 flying bomb and the V2 rocket. They were Hitler's 'secret weapons', the more feared because they had no particular target and V2s were almost impossible to destroy. Radar was at the forefront of the Early Warning System.

In 1944 Joan Enguell was posted to Ringstead, near Weymouth, 'where a

B Watch, Radar, with some kittens at Patrington, 1944 (Vera Webb)

highly secret receiver had been installed, which we were required to operate for no more than half-an-hour at a time, as we stared unblinkingly at the tube. The launching pads, which had been discovered across the Channel, were expected to disgorge their rockets at any time, and it was hoped we could plot them. In the event the V1 buzz-bombs arrived first!'

After they started to arrive, Hazel Williams 'used to plot the buzz-bombs in the Ops Room, and we could actually hear them overhead at the same time. I was on duty when the first V1 was plotted, and had to shout "Diver, Diver" – the code-name for those pilotless craft! [The RAF also operated what were called 'Diver Patrols' to destroy or tip over these flying bombs.]'

In her weekly diary Jean Young, a Radar Operator, followed the progress of the war. She observed impersonally on Friday 16 June 1944:

> The Germans have produced their secret weapon – pilotless planes. They have been used several times now, in increasing numbers both by day and night. They sound distinctly unpleasant – sort of torpedoes with an engine, and there is a terrific blast when they crash. They have a charge in their nose, so they do the same amount of damage again, after they had dropped their bombs.
>
> Sunday 9 July 1944 – The Flying Bombs have been coming over all week! Mr Churchill made a statement in the House the other day. There have been 2,754 bombs so far, and 2,752 deaths with 8,000 injured. Our fighters are shooting down a lot and they have brought up a terrific Balloon Barrage outside London.
>
> Friday 22 September 1944 – The new idea with the Flying Bombs is to launch them from the planes – but there haven't been very many. We had some go right over us here! There *are* some rockets – V2s – coming over London, but nothing is being said about them yet.

At the receiving end Nita Goldsmith describes what happened when 'a doodle-bug fell in the garden behind our living quarters at Keston, just after Domestic Night and cleaning inspection. One girl, who had missed her tea to have a bath, was more concerned about the loss of precious hot water when the plug was blown out, than the fact that the plaster from the ceiling had rendered it useless.'

An amusing story is told by Kay France, who was an Admin Sergeant in a WAAF Hostel in London which was used by airwomen working at Air Ministry, the War Office and other offices:

> At about 11 a.m. there was a terrific explosion, instantly recognized as a

Sperry Equipment, which was used to calculate Flying
Bomb positions, exhibited at Rootes, Piccadilly,
November 1944 (Naomi Fillery)

nearby hit by a V2. The building shook, there was a great roaring noise like
a train, a sound of crashing glass and then silence for what seemed ages, then
a muffled screaming started up. It was just one voice. We traced it to a
bathroom of a corner apartment at the end of the corridor.

The door was locked. I sent someone for help and two Corporals arrived
within minutes with fire axes and broke the door down. As soon as it was
opened, water gushed out over our feet, window glass lay everywhere and
the bath was upside down. It was from underneath this that the muffled
screams were coming. The two policemen heaved it up and under it lay one
of my girls, stark naked, eyes closed, screaming, but unhurt!

For a minute, apart from her voice, there was silence. Then somebody
started giggling, which set us all off. She stopped screaming, crawled out, got
up on her feet and said, 'What the hell happened?' Then she suddenly
realized that she was standing naked, with two men staring at her, still
holding the bath up . . . It was a miracle that she was unhurt, except for her
dignity, and eventually, even she saw the funny side of it!

At Winterton in late 1944 Jean Williams had a really unnerving experience.

She and a friend were '180 feet up an aerial tower, hand-turning the aerial after a power failure prevented the automatic gear from operating. Then to our horror there were two doodle-bugs, off course, coming straight towards us! Our relief, when they went by, one on either side of the tower below us, can be imagined!'

Bravery takes many forms – some quiet and inconspicuous. Tribute must be paid to this other kind, which was not uncommon among airwomen during the long dangerous days of war.

During the night raids on London in 1940, Vera Shaw and those of her watch 'were all plotting busily at Uxbridge, when one was called and told her sister had died in a raid and that she was required to go for identification purposes . . . She returned to her work, white-faced, shattered and stunned, but continued plotting. As dawn broke and the first trains started, she went wearily and sadly up to do the identifying. A truly brave person!'

11
FROM THE NILE TO THE GANGES

The first WAAF to go abroad were the Code and Cypher Officers, who were sent to the USA in 1940. Others followed afterwards to process the increasing volume of Signals traffic which grew rapidly as America was drawn into the war.

On board the ship – which had been rerouted to Canada – for her American post in Washington, Florentia Tudor stopped to chat with another very seasick WAAF. 'As she hadn't eaten for some time, I offered her some of my chocolate ration and was amazed when she scoffed the lot!' Another 'very hungry, butch

Code and Cypher Officers, bound for the Middle East, off the west coast of Africa, August 1941 (Doreen Morle)

Code and Cypher Officer having a before-breakfast walk around the deck, when asked how she was, replied, "I'm ravishing!"'

The nearest that Stella Cottman came to foreign parts was Northern Ireland, and although it was for Home Forces it still meant a sea crossing in which she wished herself dead! On her first posting at Kilkeel she found 'the Mountains of Mourne very beautiful and we walked a lot'. At Downhill

there was a ferocious, wild billy-goat up the slope above the village, who sometimes came down to check up on passers-by and took to charging all he didn't like. I remember an airman leaving the pub, who had to chase the Bedford van all the way up the hill with Billy in hot pursuit. He was very glad to be hauled over the tailboard by his collar when he finally caught up with it, fortunately still ahead of Billy!

Then, using new 10 cm equipment, she was posted to Ballywalter, which 'was in

Airwomen outside their tent, called Dim View, in Egypt (Kay France)

a boggy meadow on the seashore. As Corporal in charge of a new Radar site, I reported that our Radar equipment was working, but the ablution block was not completed – the shiny new toiletwear not being connected to either water or plumbing of any sort!'

Stella Buist, sitting at home, was highly envious of her pilots' freedom to go abroad:

> As each day passes, oft we sit and sigh,
> Thinking of those happy days gone by,
> Before you went away to lands afar,
> To fly your Beauforts 'neath an alien star!

She need not have been too envious, for in March 1944 airwomen at last found their way abroad. Joyce McKay declared, 'if my name wasn't the first down in volunteering for overseas, it was only because I didn't see the notice first!'

The earliest volunteers, carefully selected, medicated, lectured and equipped, finally set sail for Egypt, although they themselves had no idea of their destination, so secure was the blanket of secrecy surrounding their departure. All they knew was that they were embarking on an overseas posting and that was enough for them! Egypt was, with very few exceptions, the posting most enjoyed by the girls, and it was here that the majority of wartime WAAF served.

In 1944, while Anne Pike was stationed at Heliopolis, Cairo:

Technicians were working on a German Junkers 52, brought in from the blue. After servicing, a South African pilot and a couple of Technicians were taking it up for a test. I was asked if I would like to go along and, young and daring, I said 'Yes'. We took off and the noise inside was terrible. I had to sit on the floor as the inside of the plane was just bare. As we flew, the desert stretched for miles and miles beneath us. Afterwards, as I left the aircraft I had a good look at it, and I'm sure one of the galvanized wings was longer than the other!

When she first arrived at Port Said, Margaret Furness was immediately struck by the smells:

Egyptian cigarettes, cheap petrol, unwashed humanity, exotic perfume, jasmine and frying chippattis – wonderful!

Later, while I was stationed at Heliopolis, they had the worst sandstorm for

Four airwomen of Tent B7 cleaning up the desert at 22 Personnel Transit Centre, Almaza, Egypt, December 1945 (Margaret Furness)

Sitting on the step outside a tent at Almaza, December 1945 (Margaret Furness)

sixty years. The temperature rose to an abnormal level, and we three girls plastered night-cream onto our faces, to keep our skin from drying out. When the sandstorm struck and we struggled outside to grapple with the guy ropes and tent pegs, we realized that our faces were covered in grit, like pebble-dashed walls, and of course the water was cut off, so we had to stay like that for the rest of the day! Most of the tents were whipped away and the noise was like the moaning of banshees – really unnerving!

Despite the discomforts, the airwomen made the most of such postings. 'I went to Luxor and Aswan,' says Eileen Morton, 'saw the temples, the Valley of the Kings and Tutankhamen's tomb – places I would never have seen as an ordinary working girl.'

Airwomen were withdrawn from Telecommunications Middle East, late in the war and only returned just after the war. Kay France describes the conditions:

Accommodation for the first contingent of airwomen – living quarters are a square hole dug in sand, baked hard by continuous wetting and drying, with two steps down in local bricks, and tent on top, lit by hurricane lamps. Two iron beds are allocated to each tent. These were directly opposite the men's

A trip to see the Pyramids on Christmas Day 1945 (Kay France)

tents, with no boundary fence, no office accommodation and only one small brick hut with two cold water showers and two bucket-type lavatories in it. Dining facilities were in a large marquee tent.

Christmas Day 1945 – an organized trip to see the Pyramids!

I had approximately 100 Signals WAAF for Telecommunications Middle East. The girls were to take over from wartime RAF personnel, awaiting repatriation to UK. TME was about 5 miles into the desert from Heliopolis, and underground. Morale was low, working conditions terrible and discipline non-existent. Our Flight Sergeant Faultley (affectionately known as Ma) – about forty, large and jolly – soon got things sorted out work-wise. I had accommodation, welfare and the admin side to sort out.

TME – 1st day. Saw Station Commander. Told him I wanted WAAF Quarters fenced into a compound, a solid-built Guardroom and Office with sleeping accommodation for two, and at least three huts of some sort for the

Explaining to the Chicos how to clean the camp
septic tank (Kay France)

Foreman of the WAAF camp with two of his
helpers (Kay France)

Duty Corporal in her new Administration Office
(Kay France)

Kay, with guard-dog Tony, against the perimeter
fence (Kay France)

Signals workers. I also asked for some daily labour to keep the compound and ablutions clean. He passed me on to the Foreman in charge of the local labour gang, an Egyptian who spoke English, with instructions to get everything I wanted done at once. I had been briefed on the Egyptian attitude to women, so had to make my demands rather forcefully. Next day gangs of Arabs arrived and a fence was erected. Within days I had a brick Guardroom and Office. Then an old Sudanese, who spoke English, reported to me with two boys and there were another two of about twelve years. It was sign language at first, until we learned a bit of each other's language. Abdul, the Sudanese, I put in charge of the boys, who were all Abduls or Achmeds by name. To avoid confusion, I called them all Chico and gave them the numbers 1–6. They thought this was hilarious and at first tried all sorts of tricks by swopping numbers. So I started a points system, with a weekly bar of chocolate for the Chico with most points!

The Admin Office operational at last, complete with Duty Corporal.

One of my early requests had been for improved conditions regarding the lavatory bucket system. The 'flush' went into a tank sunk into the floor of the block and should be emptied and disinfected weekly. It was done by the

A new sleeping hut for the Signals Shift WAAF (Kay France)

Heliopolis – inspecting the temporarily employed WAAF Palestinian recruits from Training Centres at Lydda, 1943 (Shirley Edwards)

Chicos, finishing with a thorough bath in an oil drum, which the Chicos thoroughly enjoyed!

Interior of one of the huts built for the Signals Shift workers – spartan, but more comfortable for working and sleeping on a four watch system. Iron beds had three biscuit-type mattresses. Bedspaces had a shelf over, with hooks under to hang things. Bomb boxes at foot stored all other possessions. Windows of fine wiremesh for ventilation. I later managed to get ceiling electric fans installed and curtains for all shelves to keep them free from sand. Each of four huts had a Corporal's bunk (room). Eventually all airwomen moved into the huts, leaving tents empty. Thirty locally enlisted Palestinian girls were delighted to live in the tents!

The camp was guarded by the Royal West African Frontier Force – all 6 ft tall West Africans. I was also advised to get a Guard Dog. One was delivered, filthy, brown, wild and hungry, having been shut in a crate on the road for a week. I fed him and put him under a shower and he turned out to be white with black patches. I called him Tony, because he came from an Italian prisoner of war camp, and he never left my side, day or night. I trained him to growl and bark when the Guards approached me at night, and to seek out and bark when the Chicos hid in an empty tent for a sleep! Security fence in background at least gave privacy.

There was a man-made garden at the front of the Warrant Officers' and Sergeants' Mess. Tons of soil had been brought and dumped on the sand, to a height of about 5 feet, before the end of the war. When we arrived it was a blaze of colour with flowers, shrubs and trees full of blossom. The pool even had a goldfish. This oasis was surrounded by sand, sand and still more sand!

The coolest place at midday was the covered verandah of the Mess, looking out onto the beautiful man-made garden. When we WAAF arrived, there were about fifty RAF members, so it was rather a shock to them to have three WAAF SNCOs disturb their bachelor existence.

One of a convoy of lorries, complete with POW drivers and MT Warrant Officer, on the way to Alexandria (Kay France)

A house in Alexandria had been taken over as a Leave Centre for WAAF in the Cairo area. Part of my duties was to do monthly checks, which entailed an uncomfortable 12-hour journey. I soon found there was a regular convoy once a month doing the 80 miles to a Maintenance Unit near Alexandria from our camp. The MT Officer was a Warrant Officer in our Mess and drove the first lorry. The other drivers were German prisoners of war. Halfway, the only building on the whole road was a wooden hut, where an Arab sold warm beer and lemonade. The toilet was a pit in the sand with a matting fence.

To her shame, Joyce McKay doesn't remember too much about her work at the Pay Office in El Gedida, Heliopolis:

I do know it was deadly dull – scrutinizing other people's figures and sums for mistakes, which doesn't say much for the way jobs were allocated, as I could never myself add up! I used to drowse away many an Egyptian afternoon!

After this I went to Petah Tiqwa in lovely Palestine. I remember those

Break for food in Tel-Aviv in 1945 (Barbara Kirkham)

banana and orange groves in the morning and the scent of mimosa in the evening. I suppose no later exotic holidays can equal the thrill of discovering the world when one is young!

Palestine did not hold such pleasant memories for Minnie Hodges. 'I nearly drowned in Tel-Aviv. I was standing near a groyne, when a great wave swept over me and carried me away. I had given up, when I saw my mother's face in the water, which made me fight to save myself. By then the RAF and lifeguards had come to my rescue and I was dragged out!'

India was another late but exotic posting. In October 1944 Pamela Cuthbertson arrived at New Delhi with the first contingent of airwomen: 'The men were wonderful to us, took us out and made us feel good. My friends were excellent. We never felt lonely. Work in the Equipment Stores was so enjoyable and everyone worked together.'

In 305 Maintenance Unit, Bombay, 1945 (Mary Ker)

On 15 June 1945 Betty Thomson was writing:

So hot – 115 degrees! Oh for the monsoon to arrive! Fans just move the air around. Spent most of the day checking portion of pilot's Route Books for new airfields opened up as Japs retreat. Coolies throw water at bamboo screens to cool the air – unsuccessful! Missed transport back at 6 p.m. Took Tonga. Flying foxes are dark shapes flitting from tree to tree. My tin bath full of hot water. Bed under mosquito net. Roll on leave!

Soon airwomen went beyond India to Ceylon, which received mixed reports. For Catherine Pearson, 'the journey from Bombay to Delhi in 1944 was an eye-opener – hard seats, heat and flies. We all enjoyed the fruit though. Then came the flight from Delhi to Colombo, sitting on the aircraft floor, and being met by the Press when we landed.'

An early arrival at Kandy, Pamela Crump found, 'we had no home comforts. One tap of water for twenty and deep pit latrines. There were twelve-year-old boys to look after us, but nevertheless it was a very happy station!'

While Joan Raine was in Ceylon she heard

that the ceremony known as the Perahera, or Parading the Tooth of Buddha, held every few years, was to take place in the capital, Kandy, in August 1945. So my friend and I decided to travel the 80–100 miles from Colombo to Kandy, watch the procession and return on the overnight mail train, ready for duty next morning. Another friend sought permission from our WAAF Officer and was refused, but Anne and I just went!

The festival was magnificent! Forty-eight elephants, all beautifully decorated, paraded through the streets of Kandy. The procession included the beautiful Kandyan dancers, who accompanied the splendid casket containing the Tooth of Buddha. The shopkeepers brought out boxes for viewers to stand on. It was while we were securing a good viewing position that I happened to glance to my right, and there was our WAAF Officer who had refused permission to our friend. I whispered hastily to Anne and we tried to melt into the crowd, making ourselves as inconspicuous as possible and making sure that we got ourselves to the railway station in good time for the overnight train for Colombo. For this there was the usual mad scramble from the local travellers, and we were very cramped and not very comfortable on the wooden seats. Later, a kind Group Captain spotted us and invited us into his very roomy and comfortable first-class compartment.

At the end of 1945 many WAAF were transferred from Ceylon and India to Singapore. One of the first to arrive was Pamela Crump, who was far from happy. 'This is our Headquarters by the sea, with our beds in Tanglin Barracks. Everything was filthy, just as the Japanese had left it. No means of cooking except oil and water. Had no bread – just biscuits and tinned pilchards!'

One of the last wartime postings for airwomen was Algiers, as the WAAF Director feared its moral influence. This was a feeling not shared, for the most part, by the girls who were sent there.

After three years at Aldergrove, Edna Murray was posted as Corporal, first to Egypt and then to Algiers. Describing a typical day, she found

Algiers Bay a wonderful sight and plenty of fruit! A gharry with open sides collected us at 7.30. Off through the gardens – trees loaded with citrus fruit. A drive through Algiers to the coast road and to 351 MU, where I spent the day dealing with equipment problems. Tiffen (lunch) supplied there. Back to hotel for 5 o'clock dinner. Then we go out, providing a British or Allied serviceman signed us out and back. Always plenty of dances and socials at Service Units.

Three girls in Algiers, 1945 (Joan Davis)

On her short posting to Algiers, Winifred Burnett was most impressed by 'the sunlight and bright colours, which were such a lovely change after the drabness of Britain!'

After six months, however, the airwomen were recalled, much to their regret.

Some time after the successful invasion of Sicily and then Italy in the summer of 1943, WAAF appeared there in small numbers. An early arrival was Yvonne George, in her capacity as Intelligence Officer:

The war in Italy was progressing and we followed by lorry. At Forli, the town mayor allotted as our billet the Lucretia Borgia Museum, filled with priceless furniture, paintings and other valuables, most of which we stored in two large rooms.

As the only female member of the unit, I took possession of the Music Room, a small beautifully oak-panelled room, with lyres and lutes hanging on the crimson damask walls, and small diamond-latticed windows. My service camp-bed faced the door, over which was a large painting of Cesar Borgia, Lucretia's murderous brother. He had black hair, a full black beard, dark piercing eyes and wore a black doublet with a huge white ruff.

I swear the room was haunted, as often in the middle of the night I would wake up to hear strange creaking noises, resembling groans. On one particular night of full moon, I was absolutely terrified, but dared not cry for help for fear of the derision of the fourteen Army men, and me the only member of the RAF!

One night I was taken to see what a modern battlefield looked like. We climbed to the top of a hill and there below us was a scene I had never expected. There were the Allies and the Germans dug in, facing each other, with no-man's-land sandwiched between. Both British and German troops were using powerful floodlights, which rose up to the sky like an archway. There were a few sporadic shots, but it was most uncanny! Obviously I was lucky to be there on a quiet night!

The first servicewomen to land in France after D-Day were airwomen, specially trained as Flying Nursing Orderlies to accompany casualties being evacuated by plane back to the UK.

Based at Blakehill Farm, Bonney Budd recounts in her diary for 10 September 1944 a rather unusual day in her work on one of these Air Ambulances:

The return of Corporal Lydia Alford, one of the first three Nursing Orderlies to land in France on D-Day +7 to air evacuate casualties back to the UK, June 1944 (Joan Crane)

Dawn rise. Aircrew breakfast – bacon and eggs. Check equipment, oxygen etc. and get flasks filled and sandwiches from kitchen. Take off first light and land at West Zoyland to pick up supplies – clothing, boots, sweets, rum and milk. Told to land at emergency airstrip near Nancy (France). No other planes there except a Spitfire under repair by the pilot. Told to phone Headquarters and ask for Major Miller Munday. He told me to pick up Colonel Frank and his men, who would not be ready until the following morning. I had to make my own arrangements, and the Spitfire pilot told us of an American hospital down the road, evacuating wounded from Italy. He told us if we heard tanks to take cover, as there were Germans still about! We had to, but fortunately they were French tanks! Made very welcome by Americans, but as there were no women there, I had to sleep in the CO's tented office, escorted by a guard. The Americans took us to the plane next morning, where Colonel Frank and his men were waiting. They had to be kitted out from our stores, as they had been behind enemy lines! Colonel Frank was only slightly injured and declined my attention. Flew them back to West Zoyland, where we had dinner, and then to Blakehill Farm – a long trip!

Shortly after Bonney's visit, the first contingent of WAAF to go to work in Europe after D-Day arrived. 'We became known as the "Fighting Forty-Five",' says Jean Brown. 'Handpicked, we were told at Kirby – the cream of the cream of the WAAF, ambassadresses for our country – 2 Officers, 4 NCOs and 45 airwomen!'
Rusty Woodin, also in the party, takes up the story.

We were due to go on Friday 15 September 1944 by Dakota aircraft, but these were frozen for use in the Arnhem landings, so we were sent by sea on Monday 18 September 1944 instead.
After Southampton and Spithead we were put in the hold of a Landing Ship

The 'Fighting Forty-Five' on board a troopship at Southampton, heading for France, September 1944 (Gilchrist Brown)

The first contingent of airwomen in France after D-Day getting their tents ready in an orchard, September 1944 (Gilchrist Brown)

Infantry, which was actually the Belgian cross-channel steamer *The Princess Astrid*. What a night we spent! It was not the enemy we were afraid of, but the cockroaches, which milled around the stairs like Piccadilly Circus. What a relief it was when morning came and we went up on deck. We were in a big convoy, balloons flying, the sea a magnificent blue and white! What a sight!

As we came closer to Arromanches, we transferred to a Landing Craft Tank, and as we approached Mulberry Harbour there was a hushed silence as everyone spotted the hundreds of German prisoners of war on the quayside . . .

We had a fantastic welcome from the other services and then travelled to our camp, which was in the grounds of a house called *Bon Accueil*. We slept in tents in the orchard – apples used to drop on the tents and chickens clucked outside. The offices were in a cider factory – primitive but clean. I shall always remember a little old French lady in black, who sat on a seat outside the *Bon Accueil* crying – it was her home!

We could only go a short distance outside, as the sides of the roads were mined.

We were in Normandy about ten days and then flew to Gent in Belgium. When we arrived, fighting was still going on in Blankenberge and other pockets, and you could hear the gunfire.

We were given a tremendous welcome by the Belgian people, and invited to their homes – flags everywhere! We worked long hours, but there was plenty to do in our free time. Our first Christmas was bitterly cold and we had very little heating. Frost formed on our hair as we marched to the office in the morning!

Then came New Year's Day 1945, and the breakthrough in the Ardennes by the German Army. All the RAF airfields on the Continent were attacked. The welcome flags in Gent were taken indoors – understandably! I remember seeing the beginning of the attack on the airfield behind our Headquarters. Hearing the noise of aircraft and looking up, I thought, 'They are peculiar D-Day markings,' and they were German crosses on the Focke-Wulf 190s! This set-back did not last long and then everything went back to normal.

On this memorable 1 January 1945 Anne Cresswell was 'posted to a Photographic Unit in Belgium. The job was to process thousands of photo-

VE-Day Parade in Gent, 9 May 1945 (Gilchrist Brown)

reconnaissance prints for the Army as they advanced into Germany.'

Meanwhile, 'based in and around Paris in 1945, before the ending of the war', Barbara Coe found that 'British rations were not too good – dried potatoes and very hard pears – but when the Americans fed us, the food was unbelievable! The French people used to raid the dustbins regularly.'

'Before we left Gent,' Rusty Woodin continues, 'we 85 Group WAAF took part in a VE-Day Parade in Gent, but most impressive of all was the Farewell to Bruxelles Parade, in which we also took part!'

Thence, the girls with 85 Group, 2nd Tactical Air Force, followed it across Europe into Germany itself. According to Jean Brown, 'I understand we were the first working party to be sent to the British Army of the Rhine to relieve men for duties elsewhere [or it might have been for demobilization]. Most of us were Clerks, General Duties.'

Rusty Woodin finishes their story:

Later in 1945 we moved to Hamburg. We travelled by train, wrapped in blankets, as it was November and very cold. When we were there, often in the early days when we set off in the morning we would see swastikas scratched in the dirt of the path, but it didn't worry us.

The Headquarters building, which seemed quite new and smart, had previously belonged to, and been occupied by, the Luftwaffe. We hadn't far to go to our offices, and all through the very cold winter of 1945 there was always a thin frozen covering of snow on the ground. The waitresses who served us in the Mess were ex-German WAAF.

Some time later at Celle in Germany, what upset Pat Bracey most 'was the proximity of what had been Belsen Concentration Camp, the cities reduced to rubble, the depressing aftermath of war and the grave of my RAF boyfriend at Limner.'

To reach these overseas stations the RAF used a mixture of planes and ships – mostly it was troopships. This proved a somewhat mixed blessing. On her voyage out to Ceylon, Rusty Scarlett found, 'we had very small cabins, which contained four or five three-tier bunks, and at night, because of the blackout, they were uncomfortably hot and airless. We likened them to the Black Hole of Calcutta – but the men were far worse off.'

On the other hand, going overseas was 'quite an experience' for Audrey Fry.

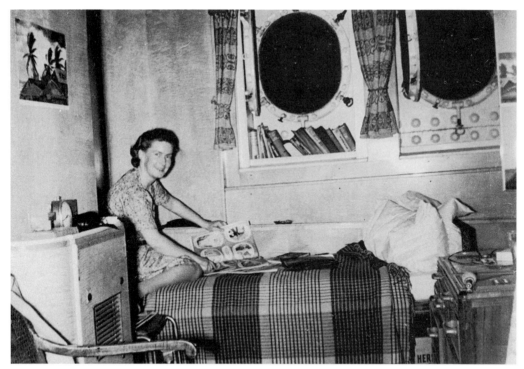

Carol occupying a cabin on the *Queen Elizabeth I* in 1944. The bathroom is on the near side (Carol Hastings)

'I sailed from Liverpool in 1944 on the luxury troopship *Britannic*. The aircrew cadets on board acted as waiters. They were going to the Middle East to finish their training. It was eerie at night-time with the ship in darkness, and the threatening presence of the dreaded U-boats.'

But the best, and most unusual posting, fell to Carol Hastings, who had the good fortune to be posted as Women's Liaison Officer on board the *Queen Elizabeth I* for the whole of 1944.

I had an outside single cabin with two portholes, a bathroom with fresh water, a telephone, an electric fire and a share in a steward. The cabin was my home for a year and two days, and in that time we made thirteen double crossings. It was almost unbelievable to have three meals a day with almost anything you wanted!

There was everything in the way of weather in the Atlantic from blue sea, calm and sparkling, to heavy seas, gale-force winds, snow, rain and bitter cold.

Much depended on the course the Master was instructed to take. Like the other four big liners, we travelled alone, as we were too fast for convoys . . . and if we were on a zig-zag course to avoid and confuse enemy submarines, we would roll on one tack and pitch on the other. If there was a 'flap' on, we stayed fully clothed. At 11 a.m. every morning we had 'Emergency Muster' instead of Boat Drill, as there simply were not enough boats to go round.

[It was an interesting life, with huge responsibilities, much worry and hard work, but the small staff all helped one another and coped somehow. On each voyage to Britain they carried over 15,000 double-bunked troops for Operation Overlord and the battles in Europe, on the return journey taking back a miscellany of passengers, including GI brides and the sick and wounded.]

After a year I was taken off the *QEI* and made two voyages to India. The airwomen were warned against not letting their emotions get too roused in the tropical heat. One girl I had to see wanted to know if there was something wrong with her, as her emotions were as stable as they had been in the UK!

All this life came to an end when I was demobbed. I felt like writing to Air Ministry and thanking them for having me, but I refrained.

12
AT LAST THE WAR IS OVER

Before the war ended, Britain was already preparing herself for what would follow. Prison camps were overrun, one after another, in the Allies' advance across Europe, and Prisoners of War started to return to the UK. Airwomen were asked to welcome the men as they were flown in. 'It was poignant sight!', writes Jean Hey, as she stood

> watching them stepping out of the Dakotas, looking bewildered. We each took charge of one man, welcomed him back, chatted and took him to the delousing centre – which really embarrassed him. Then we collected him and took him to the hangar, where the trestle tables were laid out ready for him to have a meal. I brought a plate over to my soldier charge and went off to get some more plates. When I returned, four of them were sharing the plate I'd put down! They couldn't believe they could have a plate each! We sat talking with them, but they didn't eat much. I suppose their stomachs weren't used to so much food, but their gratitude was unbounded. We were all moved and I cried copious tears later that day. Before he left, my soldier took a small replica of a German helmet out of his bag and asked me to take it for *my* kindness to *him*! I still have it today!

'We almost killed the first arrivals with kindness,' comments Lily Yates. 'I will never forget some of the sights at Seighford. Later we had a call from the RAF hospital telling us not to feed them so well!'

The arrival of these prisoners of war almost coincided with the final surrender of Germany, which was officially signed and celebrated on 8 May 1945 as Victory in Europe Day. In her diary for that day, Margaret Collinge laments her VE-Day. 'The war in Europe is over – and I am Duty Airwoman, unable to join the celebrations.'

In her letter home on 9 May, Maureen Sutton describes what she did that day:

> Well! VE-Day has come and gone! And how everyone let fly! We heard the

Donkey Derby on VE-Day at No. 3 Hospital, Televinski, 9 May 1945 (Jean Corney)

news flash on Monday night and everyone was very calm. We felt flat somehow – like pricked balloons. However, we went into the Pay Office yesterday morning and were told we could have the rest of the day off and all day Wednesday. We went to a Thanksgiving Service on camp at 11 a.m. After dinner the rain pelted down and I did a bit of knitting. We heard Mr Churchill speak. At tea on camp we had real egg and lovely chips. Then Eve and I walked to York and it does look a picture. Flags and bunting everywhere! Eve and I went to the Thanksgiving Service in the adjoining Chapel to the Centenary. We heard the King's speech from there, and then the Community Singing. Walking back to camp wasn't easy. I've never seen so many people in York! We watched the Minster being floodlit and some other buildings. They looked lovely! There were lots of bonfires and fireworks about and everyone was so excited! Most of our people went to the station dance and got to bed at 2.30. They seem to have had a good time, so that's the main thing!

As early as April 1945, Jean Young remarks, 'Everyone was afraid to get too excited about the end of the war in Europe, because the Japanese war still had to be won.' Nevertheless there was now a visible slackening of tension. On flying stations, when their duties allowed, pilots could take WAAF on a flight over Europe, as an evident demonstration of the end of hostilities and as thanks for the valuable contribution of WAAF to the RAF during the war. Such trips were often named 'Baedeker Flights', after the famous European tourist guide book!

In July 1945 Joan Schneider had an unexpectedly eventful day.

I went up in a Lancaster! This is one day I'll not forget! I sat up front with the pilot and we flew to Germany. Over the North Sea my thoughts were of dear Maurice [her fiancé, who was killed on a mission] and all those wonderful boys who are no more – I wonder what their thoughts would have been? My heart was breaking, as the miles rolled by – the devastation everywhere in my England and everywhere!

I only saw three people in Germany, walking across a field. They waved to us. Maybe they are as glad as we are that it is all over. My heart is filled with great sorrow and joy!

When I arrived back at the base, I received the papers to say that I would be demobilized in August. My heart sank!

An opportunity to fly over Europe in a Lancaster was also given to Eileen Wilson, who

Baedeker Flight, 25 July 1945 (Jean Walker)

went on a trip over Germany, down the Rhine as far as Cologne [or Köln as it is known today], me sitting by the Bomb Aimer with an awesome view of bomb craters and urban destruction. On our return journey our W/T Operator fell ill, and a request came over the intercom for someone else in the aircraft to operate the TR/1154/55 to send position reports back to base. As no one else could, I volunteered, and scrambling to the W/T position duly got through to base. I remembered that the M/F aerial should be out over the North Sea, but forgot the brake on the ratchet. The whole thing spun out and dropped into the drink [sea]. The Signals Section ribbed me for weeks about it, but not many airwomen can say they dropped their M/F aerial into the North Sea!

However, the war was far from over – a fact of which the WAAF at home were well aware! It did not need Joan Slater's Group Captain at Bircham Newton to announce over the Tannoy on VE-Day 'that there was peace in Europe, and we could be happy that it was over, but not to forget BLA – Burma Looms Ahead!' Indeed, it was in most minds. The focus of Europe had now merely shifted to 'the War out East', an area where, as Betty Wing observes, 'many men had spent the larger part of their wartime service,' and where, in the words of Catherine Pearson, 'we cannot overlook the sufferings of our men and the horrors they went through'. For men were continuing to fight and die in the war against Japan.

To none was this more obvious than to the WAAF posted overseas. In Ceylon Doreen Whyatt, a Teleprinter Operator, 'worked three watches, sweating in a very unladylike manner, while the war in Europe ended and then it was all out for the Japanese Campaign'. Working first 'in Force 136 Office of SOE in Calcutta, India', Faith Townson then moved to

> our Ceylon office, where we were operating Liberators flying agents and stores out into occupied Malaya.
>
> Our submarine picked up two agents, who had been working behind the lines in Malaya, and brought them back to Ceylon. One of them was Freddie Spencer-Chapman, who had been missing for three-and-a-half years since the fall of Singapore! After the war was over, our office moved back to Meerut and our aircraft were switched to dropping stores to Prisoner-of-War camps in the Far East.

Another WAAF doing similar work was Joyce Pilgrim. 'After our forces were

Grand VE-Day Parade, Bombay, 1945. The RAF comprises the three groups at the side, on the left of the picture. The long line of WAAF and Women's Army Corps, India, stands behind them with the huge stadium at their backs (Mary Ker)

established in France, my job was finished and I managed to obtain a posting to Intelligence at Delhi. There I worked on the Malayan invasion, which, fortunately, did not take place, owing to the dropping of the atom bomb.'

Here, also, Betty Wing was told that, 'as a result of the dropping of the atomic bombs on Hiroshima and Nagasaki, Japan had surrendered. The war with Japan was at an end!'

On 15 August 1945, after the explosion of the second atomic bomb and the unofficial Japanese surrender, Margaret Collinge in the UK wrote in her diary, 'When the Victory News came through during the night, everyone turned out into the Parade Ground. A huge bonfire was lit and we danced and sang until the early hours of the morning.'

The formal document ending the war, however, was not signed until 2 September 1945, and this was the date chosen to celebrate VJ-Day – Victory over Japan.

VJ-Day in Colombo, Ceylon (Joan Raine)

On the evening of that day, Margaret Rayworth and her friends went mad:

All the Messes were thrown open to everyone. My WAAF friend, her boyfriend and mine were wishing each all of the best, when one of the men decided to whip a car from outside the Officers' Mess. Very naughty really – but very exciting! I had to drive, being a Driver and a LACW! The Island of Tiree in the Outer Hebrides had no roads, just gravel paths and fields, so we had a wonderful time in the pitch dark.

The ride, however, ended in disaster in a deep pond of pig dirt! 'The following day there was a lot of talk about the missing car. Quite a number in our hut said, "There's an awful smell in here!" I always remember our Corporal looking at Norah and me with twinkling eyes.'

After cooking lunch for the Mess, Ivy Chatsfield went off duty at 2 p.m. 'Celebrations galore. VJ-Day. We danced in the streets of Brighton until the early hours. The final end of the war! We thanked God in our own ways. Many remembered with sadness those we had lost. My own very brave brother died of war wounds in Germany, eight days before VE-Day.'

The feelings of most people on this momentous day were probably best expressed by Peggy Peek:

> On VJ-Day, we were invited to a party in one of the large houses. I think people let themselves go, more than they did on VE-Day, as the feeling was that this was really the end of it, and we could all go home and forget about the war!

The ending of the war with Japan brought other consequences, including the opening of the prison camps where servicemen and civilians had been detained in terrible conditions – 'a living hell', as some described it.

In Colombo Joan Raine helped to type nominal rolls of men who had not survived:

> It was a very sad task.
>
> The first batch of Prisoners of War we met looked as though they were wasting away, and yet these were the so-called *fit* ones, who were only in Colombo prior to re-embarkation for the UK! The very ill ones were still in hospital. The ones we met would show us small items – a button or a cap badge – which they had saved from the uniforms of their dead comrades to take back to their families.

Catherine Pearson recalls another sad story:

> While we were in Kandy, our officer informed us that a bunch of RAF chaps, convalescing from the Burma war, were arriving, and if they visited the NAAFI we were to be gentle and kind to them. Little did I know then what a state of mental sickness they were in. When we met them I was shaken rigid! It was extremely difficult to talk to them, apart from the fact that they were extremely nervous!

Thus, the Second World War was actually over, but it left a dark shadow over many lives. The cost too had been appalling! One person out of every 150 in Britain had died; one out of 22 or less Russians and one out of 500 Americans. The Germans lost one out of every 25 and the Japanese one out of 46. Over

50 million people had been killed, only one fifth of whom had been combatants, and countless numbers had been injured or scarred for life. Whole regions of the world had been devastated, and the economies of most countries were struggling with a mountain of debt. The world was exhausted!

The following year, to lift the nation's morale, Britain held her Victory Parade. The WAAF had worked as hard as any to win the peace, but in the procession in London, as Ursula Robertson observed,

we were the 'tail Joes' of the whole Parade, with only two detachments of Civil Air Transport and NAAFI behind us. We were a little upset that we had been placed well behind the RAF, with the Observer Corps, the Nursing Service and the Voluntary Aid Detachments in front of us. Then our pride getting the better of us, we had to admit that the best *had* to come last!

Mary Allsop was the marker and remembers having

ten days very intensive training at Halton before going to Bushey Park, Richmond, for the three days prior to the Parade. We marched twelve abreast, apart from splitting into sixes to pass the Cenotaph. When swinging round behind Admiralty Arch, we couldn't understand why so many Military Police were waiting. Apparently there had been a big mix-up earlier, but of course the WAAF marched proudly on with no mistakes!

That night Ursula Robertson returned to the huge crowds

to see the royal family arrive by barge at the Houses of Parliament for a fireworks display. London was alight and the Royal Standard broke over the House. Then, *with* the crowds – you couldn't go against them – on to Buckingham Palace to cheer the royal family at home. The palace was lit with magenta floodlights, the balconies picked out in white, with a huge V sign from the base of the flagpole for the Royal Ensign and the Union Jack. Finally the royal family went in at 1220 and we made our way back to Bushey. We had been on our feet for some 19 hours but it was an exhilarating feeling and I think we did sleep that night!

Even as the war was ending, the RAF began organizing Educational and Vocational Training courses (EVT) to allow personnel to catch up on pre-war skills, or to ready themselves for new ones, in preparation for leaving the service – though not all knew, nor were able to take advantage of them. The courses for WAAF took many different forms. Some girls, who were engaged or married, like Ann Turner, 'went to Glasgow on Mothercraft courses to prepare us for our future life, and talks from doctors on many subjects are well remembered'. For Hilda Bell,

> a lady came and told us how to budget our housekeeping, or even in business, so as to keep within your income. We also went to creameries, children's homes, courts and a council meeting, and a councillor told us all the things expected of them. I think it would do everyone good to have the chance of such a course – wonderful all-round knowledge!

The classes for which Millie Mills volunteered were to change her life! Though she had loved school, she had been forced to leave early (as had many in the pre-war days of unemployment and poverty), 'and on EVT I learned more in six months

An outfit for Civvy Street made in an EVT class (Phyllis Moore)

than in nine years of school'. Many aircrew, together with other personnel, attended EVT courses in preparation for University in order to finish an interrupted degree or take a new one.

In 1945 Ossington was taken over by the British Overseas Airways Corporation (BOAC) to open civil air lines after the war, and Eileen Eason, who had previously worked on Personnel Selection,

worked with BOAC's Chief Flying Instructor, who was training RAF Pilots, Navigators and Wireless Operators for secondment to BOAC. It was very interesting to watch the progress of the trainees and speculate who would be selected – and the selection was very tough! Only the best were accepted. At the end of the course they had to make a long flight to Rabat Sal in North Africa. Well! As a result of these flights we used to get all kinds of lovely things: fresh oranges, which we had never seen since before the war, Turkish Delight, handbags, sandals and many other goodies.

The RAF also arranged talks and displays for airwomen to advise them on the best way to spend their forthcoming gratuities and clothing coupons. Monica Dunbar was at the receiving end of one of these, 'when John Lewis shops of London gave a fashion display to WAAF on what to buy with our clothing grant!' Winnie Smith attended one too, trying on fabulous clothes that most knew they could not afford, but they wanted to dream anyway.

Now that spring is here again, I dream, dear dream!
Of buying clothes all bright and new
In any shade but Air Force Blue;
Of wearing gaily-coloured frocks,
And tailored suits with silver fox;
Of snappy hats perched high on head;
Of sheerest stockings, sheerest thread;
And high-heeled shoes, crisp dainty collars,
That make you feel a million dollars;
Extravagant and shocking dreams, oh cruel, cruel mocking dreams . . .

So wrote Margaret Bracey, almost afraid to contemplate her demobilization. But for many this had already started before VJ-Day.

Demobilization, or 'Demob to Civvy Street' came early for some girls. The ones married to servicemen were at the top of the list, to give them time to get together some kind of home in badly-bombed Britain for their shortly returning menfolk. Others were not so lucky. As early as 22 September 1944, Jean Young notes in her diary that the WAAF Demobilization Scheme had been announced. To her disgust, she found, 'I am in Group 42!'

In June 1945, with a group of similarly placed airwomen, Sheila Purdie was the recipient of an unexpected action, indicative of the spirit engendered during the war:

We had to travel to London to get to Birmingham on our way to be demobbed. On the station platform, a young Guardsman was talking to us – I think there were six of us – when he suddenly dashed off, leaving us with his kit. Our train came in and there was the usual scramble for seats, so his kit was left on the platform. Fortunately for us, just before we pulled out of the station he arrived back, and thrust into our hands six paper bags from the canteen containing sandwiches, an apple etc. It was such a kind gesture from a total stranger to us all. He was off overseas and I do hope he survived the war.

In July 1945 Anne Turner

travelled up to Wing Headquarters to get clearance, and left next day for Gloucester to work in Records – Radar being no longer needed. I worked in this very busy office, preparing post-war credits and gratuities until 21 August, when my name was up in Station Orders for release.

I was demobbed at Wythall, Birmingham, on 31 August and issued with food ration cards, 146 clothing coupons, £12 10s clothing allowance, and two months leave with pay and ration money!

I was glad to go home, but oh, how I missed the companionship of my WAAF friends. Those years stand out as the best of my life!

For Peggy Peak, demob came a little later:

In late November my release came through with some others, and we spent a week walking around the camp, clearing from every section. Then we were off to Birmingham for the finale. That was another ordeal – the final medical, and then collecting masses of paper to send you into civilian life. Next day we were bound for home – still in uniform for the last time –

Redundant aircrew and Radar Operators at Leconfield were deployed into other sections, summer 1945 (Nita Whowall)

happy that the war was over, but sad at the parting, because we knew, deep down, that we would miss the comradeship!

There were also those who had married or planned to marry servicemen from other countries. One of these war brides destined for Canada was Mary Green:

We planned to marry in 1944. All winter long, on my precious days off, I worked on a white wedding dress, three bridesmaids' dresses and my going away outfit. Then at the end of March, all leaves were cancelled. (Later we found it was for D-Day.) Fortunately, if WAAF could show proof that weddings had been planned in advance, we were granted leave. But what was I to do without my Canadian bridegroom, who was on exercises somewhere on the south coast?

Plucking up my courage – for I was shy then – I asked to see the Station Commander. Now, he was on a par, or almost, with the Deity in our lives! Fortunately, he proved to be very human and considerate . . .

The upshot of all this was that 'Clyde turned up for the wedding!'

More problems attended WAAF who married Americans, owing to their tight Immigration Laws, as Marjorie Bradford, an Administration Sergeant discovered when helping one of her airwomen with her discharge and

the extraordinary and complicated forms. Some were 27 inches long by 12 inches wide and needed details of grandparents and great grandparents on both paternal and maternal sides.

Towards the end of the war I also had to listen to the worry of some airwomen about when it would all be over. After a few years of companionship, regular meals, clean beds and warm clothes, they could not return to life as it had been before – to conditions probably worse than those they joined up to

QEI in mid-Atlantic en route for New York. This photograph was taken from an escort plane at 900 feet. The liner was used mainly for transporting and repatriating troops at around 14,000 a time (Carol Hastings)

escape. There was also the worries of the future of those who had married (often in haste) – and in those early life or death days, who had cared?

Feelings were very mixed! As Hilda Bell expresses it, 'no more bed stacking each morning with three biscuits and blankets to fold into a roll. No more Kit Inspections or Domestic Evenings! But the thing that really hit you was parting from your friends and the other lasses, as we all went our respective ways to go "home"!'

In her diary, Joan Pearce records, 'I was demobbed on 16 August 1946. I wept a little weep for something intangible – the routine of life in the WAAF, the friends I had made, living in the country . . . I like to think of my years in the WAAF as the equivalent of going to university.' A point with which Audrey Ririe agrees, calling it 'The University of Life!'

Stella Buist writes:

> And just a word, before I close, to every absent friend,
> We've had good times together, but you know good times must end.
> Oh words cannot express my thoughts, I know not how to say,
> How much I'll miss each one of you, when you are far away!
> Of all my dearest memories, you'll always be a part,
> And I'll treasure these my memories, deep within my heart!

And what else had these girls discovered while they were in the WAAF? 'It certainly broadens the feet, the mind and the back', was Marjorie Bradford's wry comment, mindful, no doubt, of painful hours on the Parade Square and at the receiving end of the confidences and worries of many airwomen.

Some of the contrasts are pointed out by Connie Newton:

> The work of women in the other services was not much different from their civilian jobs. They did not have our unity of station life, where everything revolved around the aircraft, which you could see daily, and from the aircrew, operations personnel, mechanics, ground crew and others, all working together.

'I'm so glad I joined the youngest service,' was the considered opinion of Connie Crossley. 'We grew up with it! There were some fantastic brains and minds in it, unhampered by the long traditions of other older services.'

In many ways the girls had led a sheltered life in a small world of their own,

with its own support mechanisms, checks and balances. The uniform too was a
great leveller. Both Shirley Edwards and Joyce Grogan felt 'it made us all equal'.

From her experience of being posted fourteen times in four years, Betty Trull
deduced that

> none of us could have endured some of the hardships of service life in
> wartime but for the fact that one made some wonderful friends. We were all
> in it together. We came from all walks of life, but we had one aim – there
> was a job to be done and by heck we did it. No hours were too long, no pay
> too small. Everyone pulled together.

For Joan Schneider, 'there were happy days, very sad days of wonderful
courage, love and companionship, and some of the greatest people I have ever
met in my life, before or since'.

'One thing I noticed towards the end,' recalls Winifred Smith,

> although we were so young, we were so old and, shall I say, wise. We were
> old campaigners. The laughter we all shared, but it was the kind of laughter
> that never reached our eyes – we had shared too many sorrows together.
> Most had preferred to stay among friends on our station, rather than take the
> usual way of posting off to a strange station. Others had found a new love,
> but we had to work too hard for much time for romance. I turned down a
> commission until such time that it could be in my own trade. It never came!

A similar reaction comes from Margaret Green. 'On the whole I think we
learned to suppress our emotions because so much worse was happening to
others. We were ordinary people in an extraordinary situation, behaving in a
reasonable British manner.'

Many girls, who had enlisted or enrolled in their teens, had lost their youth, but
now they were leaving as grown-up mature young women. They had learned the
hard way to adapt and acquire confidence in their own abilities. They had become
responsible, self-controlled and considerate of the feelings of others, however difficult.

Looking back in a nostalgic mood, Barbara McMaster's thoughts

> strayed to those dark days of 1940 – the victories and the traumas. There were
> so many of us girls in Air Force Blue, spread over a vast area of supportive
> work with the men. Those eager young men dancing with us . . . Then the

realization that they would not be doing so again! The disfigurements and the long years of recovery! The incessant beat of Glen Miller as we lay on our beds, listening to the never-ending drone of bombers crossing the coast – British and German! The doodle-bugs! The rockets coming without warning. So many memories and such pride to have been part of it all!

For Kathleen Taylor,

it was the happiest time of my life! I shall always treasure my memories: the smell of high-octane petrol and greasy dungarees; the vastness of an airfield at night when I was on night flying duty; the shudder of a Wellington as the engines warmed up; the games of darts and cricket while we waited for the planes to come back – and most of all the companionship – how I missed it in civvy street!

POSTSCRIPT

The end of the Second World War was not to be end of the WAAF. Three years later, in 1949, those girls who had extended their service and stayed were given the option of continuing into a new Regular Force – the WRAF – the Women's Royal Air Force.

In 1994 the WRAF completely merged with the RAF to *become* RAF – which it has been in fact, if not in name, for some time! It is the finest tribute the RAF can pay to its partners of this postwar era.

ABBREVIATIONS

Ack-Ack/AA	–	Anti-Aircraft Guns
AG	–	Air Gunner
AOC	–	Air Officer Commanding
ATA	–	Air Transport Auxiliary (Ferry Pilots)
ATS	–	Auxiliary Territorial Service (Army Women)
BOAC	–	British Overseas Airways Corporation
CB	–	Confined to Barracks
C of E	–	Church of England
CO	–	Commanding Officer
DC	–	Defence Corps
DFC	–	Distinguished Flying Cross
DI	–	Daily Inspection
ENSA	–	Entertainments for the Services Association
GD	–	General Duties
GI	–	American Serviceman
M/F	–	Medium Frequency
MO	–	Medical Officer
MP	–	Military Police
MU	–	Maintenance Unit
NAAFI	–	Navy, Army and Air Force Institute
NCO	–	Non-Commissioned Officer – Corporal
OD	–	Other Denominations
OK	–	All right?
Ops	–	Operations
PBX	–	RAF Telephone Exchange (Private Branch Exchange)
POW	–	Prisoner of War
PPI	–	Position Plan Indicator (Radar)
PRU	–	Photographic Reconnaissance Unit
RDF	–	Radio Direction Finding (Early Radar)
ROC/OC	–	Royal Observer Corps
R/T	–	Radio Telephone(y)

SASO	–	Senior Air Staff Officer
SD	–	Special Duties (Plotter)
SGO	–	Station Gunnery Officer
SNCO	–	Senior Non-Commissioned Officer – Sergeant, Flight Sergeant, Warrant Officer
SP	-	Service Police
SSAFA	–	Soldiers', Sailors', and Airmen's Families Association
TME	–	Telecommunications Middle East
U-boat	–	Submarine
U/S	–	Unserviceable (broken)
USAAF	–	United States Army Air Force
WAAF	–	Women's Auxiliary Air Force
WAAF G	–	WAAF Officer (General), i.e. Administration
WO	–	Warrant Officer
W/T	–	Wireless Telegraphy
WVS	–	Women's Voluntary Service
YMCA	–	Young Men's Christian Association
YWCA	–	Young Women's Christian Association

INDEX

Figures in bold indicate illustrations